PREACH
INCARNA

MOWBRAY PREACHING SERIES

Series Editor: D. W. Cleverley Ford

Preaching the Risen Christ: D. W. Cleverley Ford
Preaching through the Acts of the Apostles: D. W. Cleverley Ford
Preaching through the Life of Christ: D. W. Cleverley Ford
Preaching through the Prophets: John B. Taylor
Preaching through Saint Paul: Derrick Greeves
More Preaching from the New Testament: D. W. Cleverley Ford
Preaching on Devotional Occasions: D. W. Cleverley Ford
More Preaching on Favourite Hymns: Frank Colquhoun
Preaching on Special Occasions, Volume 3: Edward H. Patey
Preaching on Great Themes: D. W. Cleverley Ford
Preaching on the Holy Spirit: D. W. Cleverley Ford
Preaching on the Lord's Supper: Encounter with Christ: Ian MacLeod
Preaching on Prayer: Monica Ditmas
Preaching the Incarnate Christ: D. W. Cleverley Ford
Preaching for Our Planet: Hugh Montefiore

Preaching through the Christian Year:
Volume 12: John M. Turner

Preaching at the Parish Communion:
ASB Epistles – Sundays: Year One, Volume 2: Dennis Runcorn
ASB Epistles – Sundays: Year Two, Volume 2: John Vipond
ASB Gospels – Sundays: Year One: Dennis Runcorn
ASB Gospels – Sundays: Year One, Volume 2: Eric Devenport
ASB Gospels – Sundays: Year Two, Volume 2: Peter Morris

PREACHING THE INCARNATE CHRIST

D. W. CLEVERLEY FORD

MOWBRAY

Mowbray
A Cassell imprint
Villiers House, 41/47 Strand,
London WC2N 5JE, England

First published 1992

British Library Cataloguing-in-Publication Data
A catalogue record for this book is available from the British Library.

ISBN 0–264–67262–3

Phototypeset by Intype, London
Printed and bound in Great Britain by
Biddles Ltd, Guildford and King's Lynn

'Sir, we should like to see Jesus.' JOHN 12.21 (NEB)

For it is in Christ that the complete being of the Godhead dwells embodied, and in him you have been brought to completion. COLOSSIANS 2.9 (NEB)

I believe in God the Father Almighty, Maker of heaven and earth:
And in Jesus Christ his only Son our Lord, Who was conceived by the Holy Ghost, born of the Virgin Mary. . . . THE APOSTLES' CREED

I believe in one God the Father Almighty, Maker of heaven and earth, And of all things visible and invisible:
And in one Lord Jesus Christ, the only-begotten Son of God, Begotten of his Father before all worlds, God of God, Light of Light, Very God of very God, Begotten not made, Being of one substance with the Father, By whom all things were made: Who for us men and for our salvation came down from heaven, And was incarnate by the Holy Ghost of the Virgin Mary, And was made man. . . . THE NICENE CREED

CONTENTS

ACKNOWLEDGEMENTS

I am grateful to Ruth McCurry, Religious Editor of Cassell, the publishers, for her encouragement to pursue the writing of this book, and to Barbara Hodge at Canterbury for expertly preparing yet another handwritten MS of mine for the printers.

D. W. CLEVERLEY FORD
Lingfield 1991

INTRODUCTION

This is a book of theological preaching for ordinary churchgoers. Some of the sermons were in fact preached to a small village congregation drawn mainly from farming people. Of necessity therefore there is an absence of technical jargon and of academic 'name dropping'. The enforcement of this strict discipline in presentation does in practice require a more thorough wrestling on the part of preachers with their theology than may be the case when 'shorthand' theological phrases can legitimately be employed. And, of course, no one has really grasped the subject until faced with the task of teaching/preaching it to non-specialists.

The sermons, however, are unashamedly theological. They attempt an exposition of the doctrine of the Incarnation on the basis that the Christian Church is committed to it, indeed the Creeds recited in public worship will not allow us to forget it. We cannot, however, explain the Incarnation any more than we can explain God but preachers should strive so to present it that their hearers can know what it is, be reinforced in their Christian faith and have their minds opened to appreciate what the Incarnation involves for the Church's life and witness.

This book begins in low gear for the simple reason that the first necessity is to capture attention for the subject, perhaps even to dispel the notion that it has nothing to do with practical Christian living. Then the preacher has to introduce the doctrine of the Incarnation at the level where the New Testament introduces it, namely a presentation of the historical man Jesus. What was he like? How did people see him? Was he an ordinary man at all? Was he merely a man? Was he God dressed up as a man? How could he be God and man? Difficult questions! Why then has the Church insisted on this doctrine? What does it safeguard? And then if the Incarnation be accepted as a paradox what are the implications for the Christian life-style?

In this collection of sermons the Virgin Birth, a contemporary even perennial subject of controversy, has neither been avoided nor given priority. It may be possible to believe in the Incarnation without believing that the Virgin Birth is how it happened. The

Nativity stories in the gospels of Matthew and Luke must however be treated with respect; where would preaching at Christmas be without them? And if they do not *unquestionably* establish the veracity of the Virgin Birth as an historical event they are congruous with the Incarnation. In two sermons in this collection they have therefore been given some serious and detailed consideration, but not first of all, and for this reason that it was the truth of the *resurrection* of Jesus that instigated enquiry into the manner of his birth. We come to know who he is first of all at the Cross and Resurrection, not at the cradle in Bethlehem.

I have had some trouble in finding illustrations to help light up these sermons, not least because the Incarnation is unique, and if some are somewhat homely and taken from my own experience I apologize. Illustrations, however, are necessary not only for the purpose of illumination but here and there to relieve the tension where a measure of abstract reasoning has had to be pursued. Preachers have to remember that for the most part their hearers are chiefly interested in people and events, not in theoretical arguments, and so the subject must be brought down to earth, but is not this what the Incarnation is about? If we cannot earth our preaching on *this* subject where have we gone wrong?

In preparing these sermons I have been indebted to too many books to list them all but I must mention two older books, *God Was in Christ* by D. M. Baillie (especially his view of the Incarnation as a paradox) and *The Faith that Rebels* by D. S. Cairns, and two thought-provoking recent publications, *Truly a Person, Truly God* by Adrian Thatcher and *Stumbling on God* by Christopher Burdon. The study of *John – Evangelist and Interpreter* (1983) by Stephen Smalley and *Christ the Sacrament* by Edward Schillebeeckx (1963) on the relation between the Incarnation and the Sacraments I found rewarding. Kathleen Fischer's book *Woman at the Well* deepened my sensitivity to feminist perspectives and how the maleness of the Incarnate Christ is transcended in the Risen Christ and the Christ of experience.

D.W.C.F.
April 1991

1

INCARNATION

And the Word became flesh.

JOHN 1.14 (RSV)

I am going to speak to you about the Incarnation. And you look at me as if I had taken leave of my senses. You have a modicum of time for religion or you would not be here now: but only if it bears on the sort of life we live in today's hectic, and often cruel world where the weakest go to the wall; only if it fosters kindness, and giving your neighbour a helping hand when he/she is down, and keeping your own upper lip admirably stiff. 'Yes, we will take that', you say, 'and we reckon we can find grounds for this attitude in what Christ taught and the way he lived. If however, you, Mr Preacher, wish to push on the abstractions like Incarnation we have no alternative but to bid you "goodbye". And if you persist we shall either go to sleep or begin planning our next holiday.' . . . Will you? We shall see.

To start with, you can't be a Christian and not believe the Incarnation. No, that is too sweeping! You can't be a Christian if you positively deny the Incarnation. So what is it? What is this that ranks so high in importance? The answer is in my text, 'And the Word became flesh', two words only in the Greek New Testament passage, *sarx egeneto*, but they are enough either to knock you down or build you up, either to collapse you in ridicule like the Greek philosophers at the very idea, or to open your eyes in wonder at what is implied. Incarnation! God in human flesh! God becoming a man! No, not simply God seen in a human being, rare doubtless but not unknown even in today's world in the self-sacrificing behaviour of some obscure man or woman in some unexpected place. No, Incarnation means God *embodied* for a time among us in this world as a man with our flesh and blood, an event utterly unique. Yes, I know it takes some believing, and even to draw out some of the implications will require more than one sermon. So let me try for a start to kindle your interest by touching on three consequences of incarnation, which may be unexpected, *joie de vivre*, pain and ties with other human beings.

1 JOIE DE VIVRE

First *joie de vivre* as the French say, or the joy of life. Here is a man whipped into hospital with a virus infection. One evening, about six o'clock, a young 'mum' visiting her father in the bed opposite brought her two children with her, a boy and a girl aged about nine. They peered at their grandad, rather puzzled, and repeated what they had been told to say. The little girl, however, was more interested in the party dress she was wearing for it was her birthday, a long, flimsy, flouncy affair reaching almost to her ankles, all pale blue like her eyes. Then she spotted the generous floor space, the thick carpet and a possible audience even if they were oldish men in bed. She began to dance. Round and round the room she pirouetted exuding the sheer joy of living. Then the boy's eye lit on the Zimmer frame his grandfather had been using to assist his faltering steps. What fun this would be! Just the thing for acrobatics! First he used it as a ladder, then to balance precariously with his feet on the handles, then, not to be outdone by his sister's dancing, he stood on his head. What was this? Surely *joie de vivre*, sheer 'good-to-be-alive-ness'. It couldn't be anything else.

Now did Jesus when a boy stand on his head? Did he walk along the top of walls when he could as easily walk beside them? Of course he did. He was God incarnate and God is life, creative, energizing, bubbling over life. 'In him was life', states the gospel of John. I tell you it was utterly impossible for Jesus to have been a dull, solemn, feeble child or man. He was God incarnate! He was *Life*. He sang as he walked the lanes and fields of Galilee. He marvelled in the flowers after the spring rains. He loved the habits of the little creatures which made up the wildlife; and he stared in open-eyed delight at the panoramic landscape of northern Galilee. Here was God the Creator *incarnate*, walking in his creation, dancing for joy. Incarnation implies *joie de vivre*. It must do.

2 PAIN

Ah, but secondly, if human flesh is assumed, if even *God* assumes human flesh, nervous tissue is assumed, sensitive material that can be seared, bruised and battered by pain. And a psyche too which is non-material, but able to be hurt in its own sphere by love rejected, friendships ruined, enemies devilish and determined, all making for a broken heart. In incarnation fatigue is taken on, and hunger and thirst, and organs which may malfunction. And of course urges, including the sexual, powerful and thrusting as is creative life. Moreover incarnation involves being netted in a family which may or may not be beneficial. Even more it may mean 'roughing it' with people some of whom delight to inflict pain. Joseph Stalin had a peephole constructed so that he could secretly enjoy watching his victims writhe under torture, and films made which he delighted to see over and over again. Incarnation means entry into this kind of world.

Please don't tell me incarnation stands for a metaphysical abstraction. It includes those hurting aspects of human existence very few of us, if any, escape, summed up in the word 'pain'. Incarnation inevitably involves pain, sometimes too terrible to contemplate. 'And the Word became flesh.' God came and lived here.

3 HUMAN RELATEDNESS

And now, thirdly, incarnation means being tied in with other human beings. It is not possible to be a human being and live in isolation. We are all *born related*. Indeed each one of us comes into this world physically tied by an umbilical cord. This is soon cut but not the physical and spiritual bond. It remains for ever, and the mother is aware of it even if the offspring scarcely is as the years go by. And other relationships of varying intensities develop as life proceeds. They have to, it is not possible to be a human being without human relationships. Incarnation requires them. When therefore we confess, as the whole Church confesses, belief in the Incarnation, God becoming flesh and dwelling among us, we must note the inference – God develops human relationships. And when we look at the life of Christ as set out in the gospels we see this happening. Jesus had fellowship with all types including 'publicans and sinners'. And if all this is true is it surprising that the New Testament does not simply assert an abstract doctrine of incarnation but tells of a mother called Mary cuddling the baby boy who caused her pain when he was born but *joie de vivre* very soon after? Please be very careful how you rub out the birth narratives in Matthew and Luke. Yes, I know the problems, but bigger issues are at stake here than historicity.

I must ease up. This sermon has already been theologically taut too long. So a story. It concerns a boy aged about fourteen. *Joie de vivre* caused him to long to go camping. He made a tent himself, a very humble affair, and of course there would be no peace for his mother till he had slept in it out in a field alone. He wanted to be tough. Nothing daunting she found a place for him five or six miles away. (What things mothers have to do!) She left him there alone with their black mongrel dog, and went home. Did she sleep? I doubt it. Did he sleep that night? It is doubtful because by the next afternoon when the sun was up, and it was warm, he lay dead asleep in his little tent exhausted. And then he was frightened. Someone was opening the flap of his tent! And there was his mother's face peering in to see if he was all right. Sixty years and more ago that was but he can still see his mother's face if he closes his eyes. He can still feel the wondrous effect it had on him. The tie is still there.

Jesus had a mother called Mary, and she had a face. We shall never grasp, even a little, what incarnation means till we stop rejecting it as a theological abstraction and begin with stories like those we love to hear at Christmas. Matthew and Luke knew what they were doing when they began there. Incarnation implies humanity in our religion. It implies 'down-to-earth-ness'.

2
GOD MADE VISIBLE

No one has ever seen God; the only Son, who is in the bosom of the Father, he has made him known.

JOHN 1.18 (RSV)

Here is a statement with which no one will disagree. 'No one has ever seen God.' And should someone presume to the contrary in his own experience, we should, I guess, write him off as a 'crank'. 'No one has ever seen God.' Not that people since the world began have not tried to get round this; that is to say they have hankered after visible deities in place of the Invisible One, they have made idols of all shapes and sizes, and have bowed down and worshipped them; but not among the Jews: all representations of God were/are strictly prohibited. The true God cannot be made visible by any kind of image. He remains invisible.

At a certain point in time however, no, not back in the mists of the remote past, but at a date marked by the Roman calendar, 'the only Son who is in the bosom of the Father, he has made him known', so *God became known visibly* It was an historical event. It happened. 'The Word became flesh' and lived among ordinary people at places to be found on a map. People saw him. They heard him. They touched him. And some wrote down their experiences. Listen to this. I am quoting from 1 John 1.1 (NEB) 'It was there from the beginning; we have heard it; we have seen it with our own eyes; we looked upon it, and felt it with our hands; and it is of this we tell.' This is the Incarnation; God made visible, not as an idol, but in a life, a human life, the life of Jesus Christ.

Now there are different reactions to this startling statement. One is flatly to disbelieve it, another is to bypass it, and third to see the real presence of God in the Incarnate Christ, or as John 1.14 puts it: 'And the Word became flesh and dwelt among us, full of grace and truth; we have beheld his glory, glory as of the only Son from the Father.'

1 DENIAL OF THE INCARNATION

First then disbelief in the Incarnation. This does not necessarily carry with it the connotation of blasphemy, nor even of atheism. There are people who profess to believe in God and to have a high regard for Jesus, they certainly would not think of denigrating his character in any kind of way, indeed they would count it most unreasonable to do so, they admire Jesus and are willing to quote some of his sayings, but they do not rank him higher than a man, however vastly superior he may be to most of us, if not all of us, being perhaps in his person the crown of the human evolutionary process.

Leaving out the evolutionary idea was this perhaps the attitude Nicodemus adopted towards Jesus as recounted in John, chapter 3? If so, it represented the cultured style of disbelief in the Incarnation not unknown today. But there were other disbelievers and their disbelief was not cultured, it was abusive. They called Jesus a blasphemer, a madman, one possessed by the devil, a sinner, and a Samaritan (a common term of abuse at the time). These accusations, however, puzzled those who overheard them. They could not see how one so impressive in his speech and in his compassionate works could be so labelled. It did not make sense. But trying to solve the problem was hard work; so they left off thinking about it. This is an attitude not uncommon in today's world. After all there is always the 'telly' to watch, the garden to be weeded and the mortgage payments to worry about. Let those who have the inclination trouble themselves with such problems as the Incarnation.

2 BYPASSING THE INCARNATION

And now the people who, while not denying the Incarnation, bypass it. For them Christianity has very little to do with history and even less to do with doctrines. Christianity is living the Christian life, and this means practical kindness to those in need, and refraining from being judgemental. Real Christianity is deeds not words, it is action not theorizing. *The Christian spirit* is everything, all else is marginal. After all is it not true that most people who would count themselves Christians are so, not because they came to believe certain historical facts about Christ of which they know very little, nor because they came to accept certain interpretations of human nature and its destiny, but because either in a community or from an admired individual *they caught the spirit*? The spirit is everything. All else is peripheral.

Those who take this line have a case. Recently there came to my notice a copy of an address given by a churchwarden at the funeral of his vicar's wife. It made compulsive reading not least because so many parishioners, and others not connected with the parish, crammed the church for the funeral till there was standing-room only, and a nearby field had to be taken over to give parking space for all the cars that brought people. Why this tribute? Not because she was a great organizer, speaker or ecclesiastical functionary, but simply because she radiated love (no other word will do) to everyone she met. When her husband, during her last terminal illness, took over her weekly shopping list he was surprised to notice the regular order for sweets, for they never appeared in the home; apparently they were for her pocket so that she was never at a loss to show kindness to some child she by chance encountered. This outgoing warmth to all she met, young and old, men and women, rich and poor was the marked characteristic of her life (of almost seventy years), and it would not be surprising if more than one mourner at the funeral remarked, 'Hers was real Christianity'. I am quite sure this vicar's wife did not bypass the Incarnation but in the light of her life even the most sincere Christians might be tempted to do so.

Then there are theologians who bypass the historical Jesus for other reasons. They draw a sharp distinction between the Jesus of history (so-called) and the Christ of faith. It is the Christ of faith, the Christ we experience notably in preaching, in worship and in our private devotions who has significance for us as we go about our lives, whereas Jesus as an historical figure in Galilee and Judaea belongs to the past and to the province of critical historical enquiry, indeed on the basis of such enquiry we can be certain of very little about him. Those academics with this interpretation are puzzling to the general run of dedicated Christians but they are alike in this that they make spiritual experience the heart of the Christian religion and not the man Jesus, not the Incarnate Word.

3 SEEING GOD IN THE INCARNATE CHRIST

And now the third reaction to the Incarnation. This is to keep Jesus at the centre of our vision. We see him. He came in order to be seen. Not, of course, that this is possible for us with our physical eyes but we must 'read, mark, learn and inwardly digest' what those who did hear, see and touch him have written down for us in the New Testament, notably the four gospels. Jesus is God made visible, which is to say more than that God is like Jesus or that Jesus is like God. In Jesus the Word became incarnate, he became our flesh. I do not say this is easy, indeed initially the very idea of incarnation is incredible. How can the eternal become subject to time? the unconditioned be restricted to the particular? To philosophy this is nonsense. It cannot be taken seriously.

And in the event itself, in the life and style of Jesus the presence of God was not *obviously* incarnate. Looking into the manger at Bethlehem people did not stagger back at the glory facing them, all they saw was an ordinary-looking baby, in so far as any baby is ordinary. The inhabitants of Nazareth did not hesitate to take their broken tools to Jesus, the carpenter, to be mended because he looked divine; and the twelve apostles, chosen by Jesus to be with him, certainly regarded him with awe, conscious that he was different, so different that only on one occasion did one of them, Peter, dare to offer him advice, and was rebuked for doing so in the most terrible terms. Jesus was a puzzle. He was like other men and yet most unlike other men. As time went on however, some of his followers began to perceive what St John in his gospel called his glory. 'And the Word became flesh, and dwelt among us and we beheld his glory, glory as of the only begotten from the Father, full of grace and truth.'

The word 'glory' is almost a technical word in the Bible. We read in the Old Testament of the Shekinah, the pillar of cloud, as it is called, which the children of Israel saw in their wilderness wanderings after the escape from Egypt, and which assured them of the real presence of God with them. The glory of God is ineffable, you stand before it amazed, you do not know what to say, the experience of it is beyond you, not least because it is a veiled glory, partly revealed, but also partly hidden. This is how it was with the glory of the Incarnate Christ. Sometimes his wonderful works appeared as clear signs of the real presence of God, at other times the limitations of manhood stood out; and at his crucifixion were there any who could see *God* there dying on that cross of wood? It was not until the resurrection at Easter that his followers came to perceive that the glory they had seen in Jesus was in fact the glory of God, the Word become flesh, the Incarnation. It was then, not before, that they had a gospel to preach. God really had been made visible.

What does this mean for you and me? It means we shall not really see God unless we make the effort to see Jesus, the incarnate Christ. Yes, we may sense the presence of God, we may stand in awe as we gaze in rapture at the glory (note the word) of some scenes of natural beauty like a sunset, or feel deeply moved, even carried away beyond ourselves by a piece of music – we may say it was 'out of this world'. To be fully human is to know these experiences but God will not be delineated for us till we turn and look at the incarnate Christ, God made visible. We need to watch what he did, to hear what he said and above all to note how he reacted to people. Does this mean that Bible reading, especially the gospels, should be an essential part of our devotion, and expository preaching the mainstay of the Christian pulpit? I believe it does. Christianity will not survive without the incarnate Christ, nor the Christian values, nor the practice of Christian charity and kindliness. We must continue to look at Jesus as well as experience the risen Christ. Christians must be his disciples, we must learn of him, never forgetting that the word 'disciple' means *learner*. Hear the text once more: 'No one has ever seen God; the only Son, who is in the bosom of the Father, he has made him known' (John 1.18).

3

FIRST IMPRESSIONS

Who can this be?

MARK 4.41 (NEB)

Here is a man conveyed to hospital rather suddenly by ambulance. This is a true story. Some days had to elapse before he could be seen by the head surgeon, since he was on holiday. Not surprisingly as the days went by he wondered, as he lay in bed, what the surgeon would be like. Then at last he was told 'He will see you on Monday morning'. Sure enough about nine o'clock on the Monday morning the ward sister addressed the whole ward with the words, 'The surgeon is on his way and wants you all to lie on your beds outside the covers'. Then through the doorway he came. He went to the other beds first so the new patient had time to watch and form impressions, first impressions. A well-built man, average height, sandy hair, reddish face (he had been on holiday), wearing a white coat, followed around by some seven or eight young doctors or students. A man very sure of himself, said little and saw much, made firm and quick decisions, gave orders and expected to be obeyed; never flustered. He gave the impression of a very successful professional who would not suffer fools gladly nor spare time for small talk. Bear all this in mind, the new patient thought, when he comes to you and he will exercise his undoubted skill to your benefit. This he most certainly did. He found no reason to revise his first impression.

1 A MAN OF AUTHORITY

Now when Jesus walked into public life in Galilee what were people's first impressions of him? What was the impact of his personality? What were the reactions of those who saw him? I want to suggest that part of the purpose of St Mark's gospel is to give answers to these questions, the first of which is that Jesus was a man of striking personal authority which caught the attention of those who witnessed it.

The author, St Mark, does not baldly state this he paints six impressionist pictures so that we can see for ourselves, all in his very first chapter. And if what he provides derives from the reminiscences of the apostle Peter as tradition says, we need not be surprised at the vividness nor at the simplicity of style as of an eyewitness account. First four fishermen, including Peter, dropping the tools of their trade for no other reason than that this man, Jesus ordered them to do so. Next a sleepy synagogue assembly stabbed to attention by pulpit preaching with authority the like of which they had never before encountered; even a mentally deranged man there goaded to cry out by the strange strength of this new voice; and yet more remarkably silenced. Then Peter's mother-in-law raised from a bed of sickness by the touch of his hand. This to be followed by the whole town crowding round the door of Jesus' dwelling hammering for healing. The sixth painting is of a man so eaten up with the dreaded contagious disease, leprosy, that the bystanders saw anger in Jesus' face before he touched him, yes, touched the leper! and healed him. The first impression of Jesus in Galilee was of a commanding figure, whether face to face with one man or woman, or confronted by a crowd, never defeated, never at a loss, but whose closest followers knew he had a secret source of power, time spent alone in prayer. This was the source and circumference of his intense activity.

2 A CONTROVERSIAL FIGURE

A second impression of Jesus was of him as a controversial figure which he in no way avoided but at times deliberately fuelled. The truth is that if we wish to delude ourselves with an image of him as a cosy, lovable creature to whom nobody could possibly take exception we had better jettison St Mark's gospel, for no sooner is he depicted there as a man of authority than he comes before us at the centre of disputes – 'Why does the fellow talk like that? This is blasphemy!' Such was the impression he gave to the religious authorities. And then this: 'He eats with taxgatherers and sinners', drawing out the retort from Jesus, 'It is not the healthy that need a doctor but the sick; I did not come to invite virtuous people but sinners'. And then the complaint that he sat loose to the religious practice of fasting, to which he protested how right it was that he and his followers should be joyful people. The trouble was he gave no impression of the kind of solemnity that was reckoned fitting for a religious teacher. Worst of all, he was prepared to bend Sabbath regulations to suit genuine human need, indeed he seemed to go out of his way to provoke hostility at this point. All in all the impression Jesus gave was at odds with what was expected. He was awkwardly different. This was the trouble. He was a controversial figure.

3 A PUZZLING TEACHER

Then there was his style of teaching. Arresting it certainly was, but for most people he did not speak plainly, he spoke in parables the meaning of which was not obvious, and when his disciples brought this matter up his reply was enigmatic: 'To you the secret of the Kingdom of God has been given; but to those outside everything comes by way of parables, so that (as Scripture says) they may look and look, but see nothing; they may hear and hear, but understand nothing; otherwise they might turn to God and be forgiven.' And if this was not puzzling enough, he added: 'Take note of what you hear; the measure you give is the measure you will receive, with something more besides. For the man who has will be given more, and the man who has not will forfeit even what he has.' So Jesus' method of teaching was leagues away from dogmatic instruction, and even further from any form of indoctrination. This might have been easier, instead he raised questions leaving his hearers to grasp his meaning if they judged the effort worthwhile. What did he mean by 'the Kingdom of God' which he so often mentioned and never defined? And why call himself 'Son of Man', what could this signify? and did he see himself as Messiah? He never *publicly* gave himself out as such. Jesus puzzled his hearers. There was the incident recorded by St John in his gospel, chapter 6, verses 66–71, when the crowds so lost patience with his words that many of his followers gave him up. Even the twelve disciples were badly shaken.

4 A CAPTIVATING PERSONALITY

Yet for all the puzzlement about his preaching his person captivated people. This constituted the problem for the religious and civil authorities, indeed more than a problem, they saw him as a threat to their national stability, such a threat that to kill him seemed the only solution; but how? His popularity rendered him exceedingly difficult to apprehend. The dilemma became evident every time there was a clash in public. Verbal traps, like the payment of taxes and his attitude to divorce, were laid by the nervous authorities, but he neatly sidestepped them to the delight of the listening crowds who revelled in his repartee, coming to see him as their champion.

5 AN AWE-INSPIRING BUT COMPASSIONATE MAN

For all the impression of authority which Jesus gave and his perplexing style of speech, those closest to him were not afraid of him. There was indeed a complete absence of fear. Awe, yes, considerable awe. Mark, observant as ever, reported this: 'They were on the road, going up to Jerusalem, Jesus leading the way; and the disciples were filled with awe, while those who followed behind were afraid' (10.32), presumably of what the consequences of the journey to Jerusalem might entail. He gave the impression of a gap between himself and people in general owing to the towering statute of his personality, and here the word 'respect' is inadequate to measure, only awe will suffice; but there was no fear, how could there be when they witnessed his works of compassion and healing on any that might be ill no matter how far off they might be from religious awareness? No one was afraid of Jesus, certainly not children. His heart went out to any that were small – 'Suffer the little children to come unto me' – and to any that were broken, bereaved or outcast. This was the constant impression that he gave. His works spoke louder than his words and when his words did speak it was because his personality breathed compassion; and if this be counted too general or diffuse to be genuine human warmth we should note how he had close friends, notably Peter, James and John, Martha and her sister Mary and their brother Lazarus. It is to be wondered if anyone was closer to him in understanding than Mary who anointed him with costly perfume not long before his death.

6 A FEARLESS MAN

No one then was afraid of Jesus, but neither was he afraid of anyone himself. He had no fear of Pilate, the Governor who condemned him to crucifixion. What passage in the gospels is more revealing on this than John 19.8–11?

> When Pilate heard that, he was more afraid than ever, and going back into his headquarters he asked Jesus, 'Where have you come from?' But Jesus gave him no answer. 'Do you refuse to speak to me?' said Pilate. 'Surely you know that I have authority to release you, and I have authority to crucify you?' 'You would have no authority at all over me', Jesus replied, 'if it had not been granted you from above; and therefore the deeper guilt lies with the man who handed me over to you.'

Dare we comment? – the truth is, Jesus loved Pilate! and for that matter Caiaphas too who had handed him over to Pilate! Had he not said in his sermon on the Mount (so-called) 'Love your enemies', a fantastic demand indeed for all of us, how can we love our enemies? but Jesus was the embodiment of what he taught.

There is a Jewish story which runs as follows. An old Rabbi once asked his pupils what was the precise hour when night ended and day began. The pupils thought hard. 'Is it', one of them asked 'when you can tell the difference between a dog and a sheep? or a date palm from a fig tree?' The Rabbi shook his head. 'When is it then?' demanded the impatient pupils. And the Rabbi answered, 'It is when you can look into the faces of anyone and see there your sister or your brother. Until then it is still night for you.'

Is this how Jesus looked into the face of Pilate, Caiaphas, the soldiers who crucified him, as well as Mary who anointed him with costly ointment? If this is our impression of him then we shall know how he was incomparable. He feared no one because as John wrote in his epistle, 'There is no room for fear in love; perfect love banishes fear' (1 John 4.18).

Who can this be? The question has never ceased to cry out down the ages, and still cries out. Is this, as the Scripture says, God incarnate? God having become our flesh and dwelling among us, an awe-inspiring figure, a puzzling figure, even an impossibly demanding figure in his uncompromising precepts, yet one who apparently cares about people, people in the mass and individual people, no matter what they have done or not done. This is God, the God we believe in, the God we worship, the God to whom we make our prayers. Who can say the Incarnation is a theoretical irrelevance? What we believe about Jesus is the touchstone of our faith and what our faith is determines what we are.

4

THROUGH A WOMAN'S EYES

'Come and see a man who has told me everything I ever did. Could this be the Messiah?'

JOHN 4.29 (NEB)

There are no miracles and no preaching in this fourth chapter of St John's gospel where this text is to be found, and no advance planning. It is about a woman who *happened* to encounter the incarnate Christ alone. What I shall attempt in this sermon – a rash attempt maybe, but I shall try it – is to see him through her eyes. What did she see? What did this one woman see?

1 THE WOMAN

Here she comes then. Watch her. A water-jar on her head, she walks steadily and upright, a striking figure, men in particular noticed her, she can't help being noticed and she knows it. But there is no one to notice her now, she is alone. She has left the town and is making for the well in which deep down is a bubbling spring. Fetching water from it is her daily chore, there was no escape from chores for her, most of her life consisted in chores, she lived at that level.

Then she saw him, at least she saw a man sitting by the well, an exhausted figure longing for water which, without a bucket, he could not reach. Drawing closer she observed that he was a Jew, she could tell by his features, and by the slight difference in his clothes from those which the men she knew wore. Then he spoke, and the way he pronounced words with an 's' in them confirmed her judgement. But that he spoke to her at all was surprising, for she was a woman, and it was not done in that culture for men to address women in public; more than that she was a Samaritan woman. This was Samaritan territory, and Jews and Samaritans had long since broken off all relations with each other, if ever they had any. Indeed so bitter was the mutual hatred that if a Jew really wished to insult another Jew he called him a Samaritan. This exhausted Jew, however, by the well, asked for help. 'Give me a drink.'

She was taken aback as well she might be. Then with an abruptness at which he took no umbrage, she said: 'What! You, a Jew, ask a drink of me, a Samaritan woman?' Instead of any kind of riposte there came the words, 'If only you knew what God gives, and who it is that is asking you for a drink, you would have asked him and he would have given you living water'. Did she set down her water-jar then and stare with puzzled eyes at the man sitting there? Who could he be? 'Sir', she began (the title slipped out instinctively), 'Sir, you have no bucket . . .' Somehow she felt this man was her superior. She could not rise to his level of conversation, so she lowered the pitch, '. . . this well is deep. How can you give me "living [that is 'running'] water"?' Intrigued, she talked on, 'Are you a greater man than Jacob our ancestor, who gave us the well, and drank from it himself, he and his sons, and his cattle too?'

2 WHAT SHE SAW

And now the question we have to ask. If Jesus really was Son of God, the Incarnate Christ, as the Church has always believed, how did this woman see him? What was he like through her untutored eyes? Bear in mind that the encounter was wholly unexpected. She happened to come across him when she was fulfilling her daily chore of fetching water from the well as she had done a thousand times. What did she see?

First a tired man, thirsty after an exhausting journey and, as she came to know, hungry as well, for his companions had gone to buy food. In short in this woman's eyes the Incarnate Christ was an ordinary man subject to the stresses of life like everyone else. It did not occur to her to think of him as anything other.

But she quickly came to see him at least as her superior. There was something about him which drew from her the address 'Sir'. Yet he was not aloof, he did not look down on her. On the contrary he knew the secret of coming close to people – ask for help from those you hope to win, do not begin by offering help – he said, 'Give me a drink'.

Then as she stood regarding him she felt herself still more intrigued by him. He said, 'If only you knew what God gives, and who it is that is asking you for a drink, you would have asked him and he would have given you living water'. But she was out of her depth. Who was he? 'Are you a greater man than Jacob our ancestor, who gave us the well, and drank from it himself, and his sons, and his cattle too?'

No, he was not easy to begin to understand, certainly not for a woman of her level. Yet she could not help listening. 'Everyone who drinks this water will be thirsty again, but whoever drinks the water that I shall give him will never suffer thirst any more. The water that I shall give him will be an inner spring always welling up for eternal life.' At that she gave up. He was beyond her. Her mind reverted to what she knew, the daily chore of water fetching. If he could help in this, well and good, but she was still respectful. 'Sir, give me that water, and then I shall not be thirsty, nor have to come all this way to draw.'

But her attempted escape down the path of pedestrian conversation was unsuccessful. He pulled her up. Suddenly she was aware of an authoritative man before her issuing a command. 'Go home, call your husband and come back.' 'I have no husband', she said. She could not hide the way she lived even if she were rebuked for it; but no rebuke was forthcoming, instead, surprisingly, a commendation for telling the truth. 'You are right . . . in saying that you have no husband, for, although you have had five husbands, the man with whom you are now living is not your husband; you told me the truth there.' 'Sir', she replied, 'I can see that you are a prophet.'

3 FROM SIGHT TO FAITH

So now we know. This woman tells us herself how she saw the Incarnate Christ whom unwittingly she encountered. It is what we set out to discover in this sermon. 'Sir, I can see that you are a prophet', the alternative word for which is 'seer', one who sees. This weary and thirsty man at the well could see through her, he could see the secrets of her heart, her profligacy and her dissatisfaction with it. And he was a Jew and she a Samaritan woman, individually leagues apart by reason of nationality and history, sharply divided over the rightful place of worship, whether the Temple on Mount Zion in Jerusalem or the Temple on Mount Gerizim in Samaria. Could this man, perhaps, see the true answer to this age-old problem? 'Our Fathers worshipped on this mountain', she said, 'but you Jews say that the temple where God should be worshipped is in Jerusalem.' He did not answer her question directly but prophesied that the time was coming when that question would be irrelevant. She caught at the words 'is coming' and expressed what faith she had. 'I know that Messiah' (that is Christ) 'is coming. When he comes he will tell us everything.' And then the truth of his Person was disclosed. 'I am he', he said, 'I who am speaking to you now.'

Did she believe it? The Christ appearing as a weary, thirsty man who nevertheless could see into her heart's desire! Apparently she did believe it. I began this sermon by stating that there is no miracle in this fourth chapter of St John's gospel but if this belief on the part of this humble Samaritan woman that this man sitting by the well was in fact the Christ is no miracle then I don't know what a miracle is! but apparently anything is possible in the presence of the Incarnate Christ, his real presence works wonders.

So there took place the miracle of faith. The woman hurried back into the town fogetting her water-jar, so bursting was she to divulge her experience. 'Come and see a man who told me everything I ever did. Could this be the Messiah?' The people found her convincing. They came to see for themselves. What is more they came to believe for themselves, and because of their faith Christ stayed with them in their town for two days, as a result of which many more believed when they heard his words. They even came to the point of calling him 'The Saviour of the world'. *Salvator mundi*. All this in Samaria of all places, among this mongrel people whom the Jews dismissed as heretics.

4 THE MESSAGE OF THIS SCRIPTURE

What has this to say to us?

First and foremost the absolute centrality of Christ. Everything turns on him, how he appeared, the impression he gave, what he said, how approachable he was and yet how apart. It reminds us that there can be no Christian faith if we have never taken any serious account of this man, never seen him (as it were), never grasped how fully human he was, even experiencing our bodily frailties, and how in spite of these limitations an arresting otherness came through. There cannot be proper Christian faith without the Incarnate Christ. It will not suffice to confess belief in the Christian ethic, so-called; nor will religious mysticism by itself avail, nor a form of philosophical idealism, however noble. It will not even suffice to acknowledge Christ as a super religious teacher, perhaps chief among such teachers. Christianity, the practical expression of Christian faith stands or falls at the end of the day with what we see in the historical figure of Jesus. Yes, there is more, there is the Risen Christ, the ascended Christ, the Christ in glory, the Christ in everyman, the Christ in creation, but if we cut out the *incarnate* Christ we have cut the tap root of the Christian faith from which the Christian ethic grows. The incarnate Christ is indispensable.

Secondly this story of the Samaritan woman underlines the importance of testimony. In a way hers was lame testimony, but it was testimony to Christ and her own experience of him. There was no theology in it. She was incapable of theology. What she had to say concerned her experience, albeit limited. 'Come, see a man who told me everything I ever did.' A thin description of Christ indeed, but it was real, and that was enough. It was enough, that is, to arouse interest on the part of those who knew her and heard her, and she was hardly an oil painting! It was enough to arouse her neighbours to come and see for themselves of whom she spoke. And when they too believed the man they met to be the Christ, her faith blossomed. This is the benediction of testimony, it not only plants the seed of faith in those who hear, it strengthens the faith of him/her who gives the testimony.

And thirdly we learn from this story that neither race, nor intellectual ability, or lack of it, nor even a shady past blocks off the approach of Christ to us, nor the appropriateness of our response to him. It was in Samaria of all places that the Incarnate Christ came to be received as 'the Saviour of the World', and the whole process began with a woman approaching a well to draw water, her daily chore. We never know how, when or where Christ will make himself known. We cannot set limits for the Incarnate Christ is the Lord.

5

REFLECTIONS ON JESUS

'I am the bread of life.'
JOHN 6.48 (NEB)

'There is more in him than meets the eye.' How often we must have used this phrase in commenting on someone we have come to know. Here is a little street in London. Anyone passing along it could be forgiven for failing even to notice the man who might that morning, with bucket and rag, be cleaning his small car. You would not indeed have taken him for a labourer but first impressions would not have told you that he was one of our chief Law Lords – 'There is more in him than meets the eye'.

I have already provided a sermon with the title 'First impressions'. In it I said St Mark's gospel provides a selection of such impressions, and how striking they are! But there was more in Jesus than 'met the eye' of *St Mark*, and even of St Matthew and St Luke who expanded his writing. The deepest reflections on Jesus are to be found in the fourth gospel traditionally, and perhaps correctly, attributed to the apostle John, though edited by a later hand. It is to this gospel that we turn now.

1 ST JOHN'S GOSPEL

First we notice how differently St John's gospel opens. St Mark's, the earliest gospel, tells us nothing about Jesus till he was thirty and came suddenly striding on to the page of history. St Matthew and St Luke, writing later and building on St Mark's work, go behind the public ministry to tell us about the manner of his birth – all the stories we love to hear at Christmas – St Luke in addition draws aside for one all too brief moment the curtain of obscurity by telling of his visit with his parents to Jerusalem at the age of twelve. You could be forgiven for thinking no writer could possibly trace his story further back than those two gospels but St John does just that. He goes back beyond them altogether, back behind Creation, back to the beginning of all things. The opening sentences of the gospel read: 'In the beginning was the Word, and the Word was with God, and the Word was God. The same was in the beginning with God. All things were made by him; and without him was not any thing made that had been made. In him was life; and the life was the light of men.' So now my phrase 'There is more in him than meets the eye' sounds trite in extreme when applied to Jesus. There was eternity in him, or as the Greek Fathers of the early Church put it, 'There never was when he was not'. And so weighty and far-reaching ideas like the pre-existence of Jesus as the eternal Word, that is his existence before his birth in Bethlehem, come up for consideration, but don't be alarmed! – not in this sermon! Our concern is with Jesus in our world, Jesus as the Incarnate Word of God, the One who could be seen, heard and touched, the touching being an important description showing that a vision is not in mind at all but a physical, historical reality, a man in our flesh, a man with our nature.

So St John's gospel shows us Jesus walking about, talking and being handled; but more than this it looks through all this to his deep significance and reality beyond. So the material becomes the vehicle of the spiritual and incarnation the basis for the sacramental. Yes, on the surface St John's gospel looks simple. Evangelists have been known to recommend it (mistakenly I think) as reading for new converts to Christianity. It is in reality the most profound of all four gospels, if not of all the books of the New Testament; for it is the interpretation of Jesus by one who had years of close acquaintance with him in the flesh and in the Spirit. St John's gospel, then, is a book which requires a lifetime to master, knowing that we shall never master it, for it is about the incarnate Christ, and no one has ever mastered him.

2 A SIGN AND A SAYING

Now it would be quite impossible in a sermon to work through the whole of St John's gospel showing how the depths of the Person of Jesus were brought out by the way the various stories are presented. What I propose is a consideration of the first of the seven signs or miracles which John records and the first of the seven great parables of his Person represented by the seven 'I am' sayings.

So the first sign. It is set out in chapter 2, verses 1–11 and commonly called the turning of the water into wine. Please do not miss the point. By placing this miracle first in his gospel John showed himself intent on proclaiming the joy, light and laughter that Christ brings in ordinary life to ordinary people. The occasion was a wedding in Cana of Galilee to which Jesus had accepted an invitation. During the festivities the wine ran out. Not an earth-shaking tragedy maybe but to be reduced to drinking water after champagne is not much fun. Jesus however put the situation right. He turned some if not all of six great stone jars of water standing near into wine the quality of which astonished those present. Need the point be pressed? The gloom was instantly banished. Everyone's spirits were raised. The room was filled with life and laughter.

A trivial incident? but reflect on it for a moment! How different an impression it gives of Jesus from the first impressions which St Mark provides making his gospel almost a Passion Narrative with an Introduction. Conflict and suffering are never far below the surface. Here however, in St John, the benediction which Christ brings, called in this gospel 'his glory', is brought out first. It was there from the start of his ministry. Jesus was not the pale and sad mystic mediaeval churchmen liked to portray, and if that haunting phrase in Handel's *Messiah* 'a man of sorrows and acquainted with grief' colours our whole picture of him it is unfortunate.

John shows us a different Jesus, a man intervening in a domestic situation when there was a danger of the fun dying down. Dare I say it? Jesus was good company. Even St Mark shows that he, Mark, was aware of it for he wrote of Jesus accepting an invitation to a grand party in Levi's house which would never have been given were he not a joyful, buoyant person on whose lips the greeting 'Be of good cheer' was never long absent.

And so the stories in this gospel tell of life and light brought to individuals. A cripple with no life that could be called life for thirty-eight years made to walk. A man born blind enabled to see and enjoy the light of day. Two sisters have their brother restored to life so that 'sorrow and sighing flee away'. No wonder all seven miracles in St John's gospel are called signs, signs of God's real presence which transforms situations out of all recognition. And this comes about because of the Incarnation. Listen to the great text again at chapter 1, verse 14: 'And the Word was made flesh, and dwelt among us, and we beheld his glory, the glory as of the only begotten of the Father, full of grace and truth.' Even in his account of the trial and crucifixion Jesus is presented not as the victim only but as the victor. Jesus was no sad Saviour, he was the bringer of light, life and love.

And now the first 'I am' saying, John 6.48, 'I am the bread of life'. Did Jesus say this? John certainly writes of him saying it in the Capernaum synagogue after the feeding of five thousand people with five loaves and two small fish. It caused offence to the hearers, such offence that the congregation drifted away, and even the twelve disciples were badly shaken. 'How can this man give us his flesh to eat?' 'Surely this is Jesus the son of Joseph; we know his father and mother.'

The congregation was right to complain if Jesus was a mere man. The legitimacy of the claim 'I am the bread of life' depends on the identity of him who is reported to have said it. It can only escape the charge of nonsense, or far worse of blasphemy, if Jesus as God incarnate is untrue. But what if it is true? What if in some mysterious way Jesus is both God and man? What if the life that was in him was eternal life? What if in him the material is the vehicle of the spiritual? Then he is 'the bread of life' and in feeding on him we have his life, however we interpret the word 'feeding'.

Bread is the staff of life and wine is the joy of life; so this 'I am' saying, 'I am the bread of life', opens up the vast significance of Jesus far beyond that of first impressions. An awareness of this is what places St John's gospel in a class by itself. On the surface it may seem to consist of simple stories, even miracle stories, but they operate as windows on eternal realities. Certainly it is a real man we see but when we look closely we become aware also of the glory of God. And when we respond with our whole personalities and say, as it were, 'Yes' to his 'I am the bread of life', we receive his life, his eternal life. All this and more is the miracle of Jesus, the Word made flesh, the incarnate Son of God. The whole New Testament shows him to us but no book more penetratingly than the gospel of St John.

I know it presents difficulties. I know the ministry of Jesus in this gospel takes place in Jerusalem whereas in the other three gospels it is based in Galilee. I know there are polemical discourses here not in the other three. I know these 'I am' sayings make us wonder if Jesus could possibly have drawn attention to himself with such astonishing claims for they seem to be self-centred, and anyway the phrase 'I am' stands for Godhead. There are however answers to these questions if we are willing to believe that he was God incarnate come to reveal God. At the end of the day when we have rightly exercised all our intellectual skills, and perhaps come to the conclusion that St John, understanding in himself who Jesus really was, put these 'I am' sayings on the lips of Jesus to express the truth about him as he came to know it; at the end of the day.

I repeat, we shall have to make the leap of faith, a risky leap, if we are able to receive the life, light and love he came to bring. We shall have to believe that he was the very Word of God become the man of whom we read in all four gospels.

I come back to where I began: 'There is more in him than meets the eye.' This is true of every man, woman and child. There is nothing so wonderful, so complex and so mysterious as a human being, certainly no piece of advanced technological equipment for it was invented by man. Need we be surprised then if the God-man is mysterious? 'There is more in him than meets the eye.' We must, however, first of all let our eyes meet him, and preachers and Christian writers have a duty to show him to us. Everything of value in the Christian religion starts with the sight of the man Jesus we properly call the Lord Jesus Christ and never lose touch with him. Herein lies the simplicity and depth of the gospel. It is rooted in the Incarnate Christ, God made man for our sakes and our salvation.

6

THE MAN OF FAITH

Since therefore we have a great high priest who has passed through the heavens, Jesus the Son of God, let us hold fast to the religion we profess. For ours is not a high priest unable to sympathize with our weaknesses, but one who, because of his likeness to us, has been tested every way, only without sin. Let us therefore boldly approach the throne of our gracious God, where we may receive mercy and in his grace find timely help.

HEBREWS 4.14–16 (NEB)

I wonder if you are the kind of person who loves an argument. A discussion, yes; people who refuse to discuss are either bigoted or excessively dull. And people who love an argument are not so much concerned with discovering the truth as enjoying the fight for its own sake. Now in these sermons on the Incarnation we are discussing not arguing. Let us be quite clear. We are not even trying to *explain* the Incarnation. This can never be achieved for it is a paradox, as I hope we shall come to see, perhaps the greatest of all paradoxes; no, we are to see, if we can, why it is that the Christian Church has consistently held on to it in spite of all the knocking it has received. What would we lose if we let it go? What firmer hold do we have of the Christian Gospel if we begin to perceive something of its implications?

1 A REAL MAN

I begin now with the human life of Jesus, Jesus as a real human being, Jesus as a man, Jesus with a nature the same as ours. Perhaps you reckon it stupid to begin here. Whoever reckoned him to be anything else? But what is this that we confess at every Communion Service in the Nicene Creed? 'I believe . . . in one Lord Jesus Christ, the only-begotten Son of God, Begotten of his Father before all worlds, God of God, Light of Light, Very God of very God, Begotten, not made, Being of one substance with the Father, By whom all things were made. . . .' Does this sound as if Jesus was a man like us? Did this figure of the Creed ever wash, dress, have breakfast, and jostle in the streets like other men? and if you could have peeped into the manger at Bethlehem wouldn't you have seen an ordinary-looking baby, whom his mother cuddled, fed and later taught how to walk? Are you surprised then that there are good people, honest and sincere, some of whom stoutly affirm that they are Christians, who will have none of these Creeds, some indeed who will have none of the Church *because* of these Creeds? These Creeds seem to these people to take away the Jesus they respect, admire and even profess to follow, offering instead a theological conundrum.

Let us leave aside the Creeds with their complicated formulae. Let us leave the professional theologians with their technical terms, let us talk instead to ordinary Christian people, churchgoers maybe, and ask: Was Jesus a man like us? Was he? . . . But what about the miracles which the gospels report him as performing? Did he really heal lepers with a touch? Did he really multiply loaves and fishes? We can of course cut him down to size by leaving them out of the narrative altogether on the supposed grounds that they are legendary accretions; or we can suggest some form of rational explanation. We could say, for example, that what really happened when Jesus stilled the storm on the Lake of Galilee was that the boat in which he and his disciples were embarked drifted under the lee of a headland where the water was calm. This natural event has been blown up into a miracle story of Christ making the winds to cease, 'Peace, be still'. My guess is that most churchpeople would reply, 'But surely he must have been more than a man!'

Can we really go home, however, on the strength of this, content in our minds? Will not this further question rankle: if Jesus was 'more than a man', if he possessed some special powers hidden in his pocket (so to speak) more than we possess, how can he possibly enter into our feelings? How could he experience, for instance, the sharp pain of anxiety about what tomorrow may bring forth? How taste the bitterness of temptation? how know what fear is? how lie awake at night tossed with uncertainty what to do? If Jesus was not really in all points tested every way as we are how can he possibly enter into our predicament? We live at different levels! Nor is there any help to be derived from asserting that he acted *as if* he were a man, when in reality he was not, he was putting on a show *for our sakes*. In other words he was *dressed up* in our flesh, and this is how he looked like a man but could also work these astonishing miracles. . . .

We find all this embarrassing. We begin to wish the question had not been raised or the discussion entered upon, for it leaves us uncertain with our faith dented and ourselves hurt. This is why at the outset of this sermon I made the strong unequivocal assertion that Jesus of Nazareth was a real man, he did not just seem to be, he was!

2 A MAN OF FAITH

Now I wish to make the point that Jesus was a man of faith, I would like to say astonishing faith. I mean this, that his faith in God was total, whereas ours is often fitful, fragmentary and uncertain. Jesus *lived* in communion with God. It was through *this faith* then, that the power of God was manifested in his manhood. The 'mighty works', the miracles he wrought as a man of faith, a real man, not a man dressed up in our flesh and blood as if he were a man, but truly a man.

3 LIMITATION OF KNOWLEDGE

And now the consequences of this. If Jesus was truly a man then he did not know everything any more than you and I know everything. He was in ignorance about some things. When at the feeding of the five thousand, for example, he asked his disciples 'How many loaves have you?' he did not know till they told him 'Five, and two fishes also' (Mark 6.38 NEB). Nor when a woman pressed on him in the crowd and he asked 'Who touched my clothes?' he did not know till the woman disclosed herself (Mark 5.30 NEB). And when in the last week of his life he was hungry and saw a fig tree afar off and came to it to find some fruit he was surprised to find it barren, he did not know it would be so (Mark 11.13). When encountering Martha and Mary weeping over the death of their brother Lazarus and he asked 'Where have you laid him?' he did not know but was asking for direction, and they gave it (John 11.34). Yes, Jesus' knowledge was limited as is ours. He did not therefore know from his earliest years, or from the beginning of his ministry, that he was to be crucified, he only came to that knowledge as he saw the hostility building up that his words and works engendered in those who rejected them. And even at the last, in the Garden of Gethsemane, the night before his crucifixion he prayed that there might be a way of escape.

Now when we think this over we can see how he could not be a man of faith if he was *not* in the dark about many things as we are in the dark, for where there is knowledge faith is not the requirement. Jesus therefore is to be seen as the man of faith in a life situation of limited knowledge, the outcome of real struggling, real testing, continuing throughout all his life.

In view of all this is it surprising how frequently he made the comment on some case of healing, 'Your faith has saved you'?, or even that startling statement at the healing of the epileptic boy (Mark 9.23), 'Everything is possible to one who has faith', or as St Matthew has it, 'if you have faith no bigger than a mustard seed, you will say to this mountain, "Move from here to there!" and it will move; nothing will prove impossible for you'. Hyperbole no doubt, that is, making a statement in an exaggerated form in order 'to make it stick', but the implication is not to be missed, faith is what makes possible wonderful works. Jesus' life was wonderful, not because he was a kind of half-god but because he was a man who never failed to reach a state of total faith in God in any circumstance.

4 FAITH QUICKENS INSIGHT

One more point. Faith operates where full knowledge cannot be. This does not mean however that it operates on a basis of ignorance, faith is not credulity, faith is not unreasonable. No, faith goes *beyond reason* not least when it has reason as its basis. Even more, faith quickens reason. It does so by reaching out beyond reason. Then it sees more than reason sees. This is particularly so in human relationships. Through the vitality of faith there is developed a perceptiveness into the minds and feelings of other people. To use popular language, such a person can 'read people'. This was a marked characteristic of Jesus, which no doubt is why the author of the fourth gospel said of him when hostility against him began to show 'But Jesus . . . would not trust himself to them. He knew men so well, all of them, that he needed no evidence from others about a man, for he himself could tell what was in a man' (John 2.24, 25). So he 'read' Peter, Nathanael, the rich young ruler, and the woman of Samaria. 'You are right' said Jesus, 'in saying that you have no husband, for although you have had five husbands, the man with whom you are now living is not your husband; you told me the truth there' (John 4.17, 18).

What have I been saying in this sermon? Jesus was indeed an extraordinary man, but extraordinary not because he wasn't a real man like us but because against the odds we all experience he nevertheless lived a life of total faith in God at all times and in all circumstances. And if he is beyond us, as he undoubtedly is, because we none of us achieve this, he is beyond us not because he is different in his humanness from us. Let me be blunt, he could even have sinned, but he did not, not because he was immune from sin, but because it was with him as it is when we say of some upright man or woman, 'he/she could not possibly do a dirty trick'.

We haven't exhausted this subject of the Incarnation. Jesus was truly man but also truly God. There is more to be said, much more, but let us *first of all* lay hold of what our text today says: 'Since therefore we have a great high priest who has passed through the heavens, Jesus the Son of God, let us hold fast to the religion we profess. For ours is not a high priest unable to sympathize with our weaknesses, but one who, *because of his likeness to us*, has been tested every way, only without sin. Let us therefore boldly approach the throne of our gracious God, where we may receive mercy and in his grace find timely help' (Hebrews 4.14–16 NEB).

7

JESUS: THE REVELATION OF GOD

For it is in Christ that the complete being of the Godhead dwells embodied.

COLOSSIANS 2.9 (NEB)

I wonder if you have ever had the experience of talking to a middle-aged man, say about fifty, and then suddenly realizing how like he is to his father, now dead for ten years or more. More easy-going perhaps but the same diligence, the same kindness, the same Christian faith, even a similarity of speech and manner, so marked that when you parted you caught yourself saying to yourself – How like his father he is!

My subject is 'Jesus, the revelation of God'. In the New Testament Jesus is called 'Son of God', that is to say he shows us what God the Father is like. Like Father, like Son; like Son, like Father. But my illustration breaks down at an important point. The man in question was like his father because his father was in part physically responsible for his birth, there was a genetic tie, a tie which carried a similarity of temperament and nature. In a sense his father 'made him'. Now nothing of this applies to God the Son. He was not in any sense made by God the Father. The Creed we recite in Church is insistent on this. Categorically it says of the Son 'begotten not made'. The description 'Son of God' is used however to assert that he is of the same nature as God the Father, or as the Creed quaintly puts it, 'being of one substance with the Father'. Nowhere perhaps is this more strangely expressed than in my text from Colossians 2.9, 'For it is in Christ that the complete being of the Godhead dwells embodied'. So to be satisfied simply to say that God is like Jesus, or that Jesus is like God, is too feeble to stand; and the illustration with which I began can do no more than introduce the subject, with a comparison and a contrast.

And now I want to suggest three characteristics of the life of Jesus as set out in the four gospels through which, as through a window, we see something of what God is like – his self-effacingness, his suffering and his love.

1 SELF-EFFACINGNESS

First his self-effacingness. Jesus never put himself forward or allowed himself to be put forward, except on one occasion which was so exceptional that it cast his accustomed self-effacingness into even greater prominence. This was the so-called triumphal entry into Jerusalem on Palm Sunday mounted on a little donkey and the tumultuous acclamation of the crowds lining the route which he did nothing to restrain. This was the only occasion of anything approaching a public demonstration. Constant activity like an election campaign was absent. There was no vote-catching, no speech making, no public rallies of supporters. On the contrary Jesus was elusive. He was constantly slipping away from the crowds, sometimes to pray. There were even occasions when he avoided the companionship of his closest disciples. Moreover he pleaded with those he had cured of some illness or ailment not to publicize his action. In a way he was the secret Messiah for he never advertised his Messiahship, rather he adopted an enigmatic title for himself, namely 'Son of Man'. There were times when this reticence exasperated his audiences. They called out, 'If you are the Christ tell us plainly'. On one occasion his brothers spoke bluntly to his face, 'Surely no one can hope to be in the public eye if he works in seclusion. If you really are doing such things as this, show yourself to the world.' And at one Festival of Tabernacles the Jews bitterly complained that they could not find him. Jesus, I repeat, was self-effacing.

And now someone wishes to ask a question. You say, Mr Preacher, that Jesus did not advertise himself, but what about those sayings in St John's Gospel, at least seven, when he declares 'I am the bread of life', 'I am the way, the truth and the life', 'I am the resurrection and the life', and so on. If this isn't self-advertisement, and a bit pompous at that, what on earth is it? It is a fair question. In reply I have to point out that none of these 'I am' sayings occurs in the first three gospels except when Jesus, face to face with the High Priest, was asked if he was the Christ. He replied, 'I am'. Now the first three gospels tell us what happened and *what was their significance* or meaning as apprehended years later. Of course there can be no history without some interpretation not even in St Mark but in St John's gospel it is extensive. So the 'I am' sayings tell us what Jesus' words and works *in effect* were proclaiming, not that he spoke exactly like this.

Jesus in public, then, was self-effacing. He forced himself on no one. Even in teaching he left his hearers to come to their own conclusions and was constantly asking, 'What do you think?' So after telling the story of the Good Samaritan he enquired, 'Which of these three do you think was neighbour to the man who fell into the hands of robbers?' This was ever his way. He possessed personal authority. He was that kind of person. He did not, however, press himself on anyone.

All this is a window on God. God is like this. He is elusive. He is not obvious. We can explain the universe without God as the creator if we so wish. Even if some so-called miracle happens, or a prayer is answered, room is always available for some other explanation, always a way out along the avenue of chance or coincidence, and God makes no attempt to block it. So we are all left free to go our own way. The light of life is clearly provided but God forces no one to pick it up and illuminate his path. He even allowed men to crucify the incarnate Christ who brought it.

Is all this astonishing? But it is true. Jesus is the revelation of God. This is why he is called 'Son of God'.

2 SUFFERING

I invite you now to look through the window of the incarnate Christ to see his suffering. Suffering was part of him. What I am saying is that it is impossible to see him free altogether from suffering, and I am not referring first of all to his cross and passion. Because Jesus was a real man, and not God masquerading as a man, he experienced suffering. Suffering is a constituent part of human existence as we know it. There is no suffering-free humanity. We all know in a measure what pain is. We are born in pain. As soon as we see the light of day we cry, and who would dare to estimate the tons of painkillers that are consumed daily by the community? Jesus, then, experienced suffering because he was the *incarnate* Christ. Not that we can specify any particular form of bodily pain that he knew. There is nothing in the gospels about neuralgia or rheumatism, but we are told more than once that he was hungry, and in Samaria he was weary from his journey – did his back ache as he sat by the well and were his feet sore? He also knew the feeling of thirst. Not much you say, in comparison with whatever some of us have 'gone through'. And dying as he did at the age of thirty-three, he knew nothing of the pains of advancing years.

Physical suffering was not in any case, I suggest, the form in which he experienced suffering. And it couldn't be a window on God because God has no physical body. No, Jesus suffered from the hatred, suspicion and plotting to murder him which was the constant response of his contemporaries. He sought to love but they reacted with hostility. It appeared that his heart broke when Judas, whom he had chosen to be his friend, turned against him, stooping to betray him with a kiss. This no doubt played its part in his agony in the Garden of Gethsemane hours before his crucifixion. It was an agony of soul so intense that it brought physical consequences; he sweated blood, technically called *haematidrosis*. The next day there followed the horrific physical pain of crucifixion and the total isolation from compassion which that lonely gibbet made visible. In the incarnation of Christ God was made visible, in the crucifixion of the incarnate Christ his suffering was made visible.

Can we accept this? Is this a view of God we are able to entertain, one who knows the feel of suffering? No other religion but Christianity has an instrument of torture as its central symbol. But can we nevertheless grasp suffering as the corollary of love? Do we not know in human relationships how love is invariably tinged with suffering? Are we then to see God's suffering as a consequence of his love?

Here is a young man growing up keen to become a doctor, so keen he keeps his mind off marriage till he has obtained his FRCS(E), a coveted qualification. He does obtain it. But a girl 'gets at him', seeing to it that other girls, as she puts it, 'keep off her grass'. She got what she wanted and a fine house into the bargain. Did his parents see what was happening? They loved their promising son. They feared for the future, and as things turned out rightly so, but they could not intervene. They agonized, and their love was the ground of their suffering.

Is this how God suffers? suffers because he loves? 'God so loved the world that he gave. . . .' He suffers as parents suffer, especially as a mother suffers in and for her children, specially when 'things go wrong for them'. This is the suffering of which we catch a glimpse when we look at the life of the incarnate Christ, Jesus of Nazareth born of Mary, crucified under Pontius Pilate.

3 THE LOVE OF GOD

Thirdly, in the incarnate Christ we see the love of God. I believe in this most profoundly for it is the heart of the Gospel. '*God is love*.' I am hesitant however about presenting it in so many words because in religion the phrase has almost become a mere cliché and in secular thought the concept of love is grossly sentimental if not mainly sexual.

In the gospels the love of Jesus is anything but sentimental, indeed it is almost ruthless. To interpret it I want to risk inventing some such expression as 'because Christ loves you be careful!' Leave that aside; but notice how the love of Jesus gave life to all manner of sufferers who virtually had no life whether they were worthy of it or not – thirty-eight years a cripple, twelve years a case of haemorrhage, blindness from birth; but no fuss, no celebrations with the cure. Imagine the champagne and the fêting that would follow such deliverance in our day. Of the like in the ministry of Jesus we read nothing, but this love of Jesus transformed people's lives, it was firm, constant and closely akin to justice; but no love was lost on those who exuded hypocrisy, religious pretence and bigotry. Jesus exposed it with anger irrespective of social or religious standing. No one could fool him and count on his indulgence.

Is this then the window through which we should see the love of God? Not that it will solve for us the hurting problem of evil but in the light of it we shall not expect God to lift from men and women the consequences of their misdeeds. God lets us pay for our foolishness. If we spoil his creation through greed we shall suffer, and not be lifted out of the calamities which it causes. The love of God, like the love of Jesus his Son, is real but there is no softness in it. We had better be afraid of it. And certainly when we see what the love of Jesus was like we can give no countenance to those theories of the atonement which suggest that at the Cross an angry God was appeased by his loving Son. The character of the Son did not contradict the character of the Father God. It revealed its true nature. Like Father like Son, like Son like Father. Jesus is the revelation of God, his self-effacingness, his suffering and his love. 'For it is in Christ that the complete being of the Godhead dwells embodied' (Colossians 2.9). What more is there to say?

8
JESUS, THE REVELATION OF MAN

'Behold the man!'

JOHN 19.5 (NEB)

A few months ago I overheard a conversation with a man who had served as a commando with the Royal Sussex Regiment in the Second World War. It was at a time when much discussion was in the air about whether or not Germans who had committed atrocities in the war, and now lived under cover in this country, should be rounded up and punished. This old soldier was strongly against it, and when asked Why?, he replied, ' 'Cos we did things just as bad', and proceeded to give examples. They were horrible, and when his hearer showed his horror, he continued, 'Well, you see, if you didn't get to the other feller first, he'd get you, and that is all there is to it'.

That I can at least understand in war. What I find almost beyond belief are the atrocities that we committed in cold blood, that is, not in the heat of a conflict but the slow torture of prisoners, sitting targets killed by bullet and bomb, hostages used as bargaining counters, the mugging of crippled pensioners, the raping of little girls, and the mind-boggling cruelties perpetrated against whole communities and ethnic groups. Man's inhumanity to man is a sickening reality we would rather forget but cannot, for not even animals would behave as have some humans. The blunt fact is human beings can sink to depths of degradation where words like sub-human are too generous. Here then is the urgent question: Can the opposite take place? Is man able to rise to heights as well as sink to depths? If so where is such a man to be found? Among the saints and martyrs? – but all have warts. Those of us however who believe in the incarnate Christ answer this question by pointing to Jesus of Nazareth, in him we see the revelation of man as he could be and in this one instance was, for he actually lived in our world, and not in prehistory but at a time dated by the Roman calendar.

1 OUR FLESH DIGNIFIED

Before we go any further let us see how our flesh, our human nature, manhood and womanhood, is dignified by God taking it as the medium by which to show what a human being really could be.

Let me give you a homely illustration. Thirty years ago a couple on an outing from London into the country saw a small house that might serve as a place of retreat from the kind of life they lived in the metropolis, and maybe a place to which to retire when the time came. It was going cheap and not surprisingly. The roof gutters were missing, the paintwork peeled down in places to bare wood, the floor in the hall weakened by dry rot, the large garden a wilderness. The man wrote it off as hopeless; but not the wife. Standing back and eyeing it critically, she declared it had possibilities, if this were done and that were done. So they checked that the foundations and the roof were sound, bought it for what today would be called 'a song' and worked at it. They have lived in it now for years, a pleasant and convenient home, all because with the wife's insight in the first place they did not turn it down.

Apparently God did not, does not, despair of our human nature as we are often tempted to despair, he did not, does not wash his hands of it. He took our flesh with which to reveal what a man could be; and that man has never been forgotten, indeed he seems to intrigue more people than ever, even if he often puzzles and even offends. Jesus Christ has never been written off and it looks as if he never will be. Seventy years ago Communism was confidently prophesying that religion would soon wither away, but it is Communism that is withering away and religion is reviving, reviving where Communism was strongest and where it sought to establish itself by persecution and wholesale social engineering. The truth seems to be that man is unable to live without an ideal greater than himself. Only if there is somewhere a man in whom all those imperfections of humanity, as we know them, are reconciled is meaninglessness in life overcome. Where, however, is such a man to be found? That is the question, the answer of the Christian Gospel – and the word 'Gospel' means 'good news' – is Jesus Christ. God took our flesh to show what man could be, and in so doing dignified it. In this way the incarnate Christ is the revelation of man.

2 A LIVING, REACTING REVELATION

Now someone wants to rise up and say, 'Yes, this sounds all very well in theory but it all seems way out from the kind of hectic life most of us experience in the modern world; rushing through the housework before dashing off to the office, jostling in the commuter train, struggling with fellow workers over the day's tasks and often clashing, fitting in a visit to the supermarket on the way home. What use to me', you say, 'of a kind of statue of what an ideal man could be?' A statue is unmoved and unmoving, unaffected by what goes on around it.

Now if the incarnate Christ were that kind of static ideal no one could be blamed for rejecting him as interesting maybe but irrelevant for life as we know it. But the New Testament, and in particular the gospels, does not lend support to the idea that there existed in the mind of God, so to speak, a pattern or blueprint of what an ideal or perfect man could be and somehow this pattern was brought down and enfleshed in what we call the Incarnation; and this is what Jesus Christ is, the pre-existent pattern made visible. The Jesus of whom we read in the gospels does not look like this statuesque figure at all. He appears rather as a man who is 'up against it' all the time. Life around him is in a perpetual turmoil with only brief patches of peace and quiet, and he is constantly having to react to what turns up. It simply will not do therefore to settle down with some such statement as that Jesus is the embodiment of love, for God is love. This is to make the living, vibrant man into a marble figure; and anyway what is love? Who knows, in today's flippant and disillusioned world where the word is so bandied about as to become meaningless? No, the incarnate Christ was a living, moving, *reacting revelation* of what a man could be and this is how we should see him if we are to learn of him.

3 COMPASSIONATE AND STRONG

Now I do not wish for one moment to minimize the deep compassion of the Incarnate Christ. He was indeed compassionate and strong. One of the most moving stories for me about him, and the most revealing, tells of a young Syro-Phoenician mother who sought his healing for her stricken daughter left at home. But there were hundreds of such needy people on and beyond the Tyrian border, and his specific mission was to Israel. He ought not to break that principle of his special calling. But he could not resist her appeal, heathen though she was. Certainly she had made a nuisance of herself to his disciples, and he, worn by the strain of his ministry, was seeking a time of retreat and quiet; but he could not, and he did not, turn her away. Her simple 'Sir, help me' touched his heart. He did what she asked. This was like him. No woman ever was more tender, sympathetic, intuitive and understanding than was the incarnate Christ. To see those undoubted characteristics however is to see but a part of him. On another day he could calmly tell his host to his face at a dinner table that he, and his religious party, were like a cup beautifully clean on the outside but filthy and crawling with vermin on the inside. On another occasion he did not shrink from 'tearing strips', as we say, from those he counted as humbugs, nor give any quarter to those who sought to attack him with verbal traps, he rounded on them, heaping invective on their heads. On two occasions at least he resisted the well-meaning but misguided effort of his family to control his actions, and more than once he was exasperated by the woodenness and lack of perception of his disciples, and let them know it. And no one, least of all the religious authorities, forgot his anger over the trading they permitted in the Temple courts and how he overturned the counters of the moneychangers and drove them out with a whip he had made. Jesus was a strong man, all his strength under the control of principles hammered out in the early days of his ministry. Yet he was not remote, he needed friends and he had them, some very close, and not only men but women too, in this category Martha and Mary stand out.

What does all this mean for us? It means the revelation of man we are given in the incarnate Christ has to be watched carefully and studied and that over a period of time. We cannot glance at him and see what is there to be seen. We have, as it were, to live with him, watch his reaction as he stands out against the shifting background of a fast-moving ministry. Then it relates to the kind of life we have to live, it can be a revelation to us.

4 THE REVELATION AND SAVIOUR

But we need more than a revelation. And so we come to the most stupendous interview in the history of the world, the incarnate Christ, God in human flesh, our flesh, standing a prisoner before Pontius Pilate appointed by Rome to govern Judaea, and wearing that ridiculous crown of thorn branches, designed to insult. Let me read the scripture which tells of it. 'Once more Pilate came out and said to the Jews, "Here he is; I am bringing him out to let you know that I find no case against him"; and Jesus came out, wearing the crown of thorns and the purple cloak. "Behold the Man!" said Pilate. The chief priests and their henchmen saw him and shouted "Crucify! crucify!". "Take him and crucify him yourselves," said Pilate; "for my part I find no case against him." '

I began this sermon by pointing out the depths to which man's inhumanity to man can sink and how in the incarnate Christ we see the revelation of what man can be. But what happened to him? He was tortured, insulted and destroyed by the authority of the day and by popular demand. Jesus might be the revelation of what man could be but it was not the revelation people wanted. They would acclaim, as they had acclaimed many times before and would acclaim many times in the future, the conquering hero who crushes whole nations with military might exploiting them for gain, but not this man! Why not? Because while he undoubtedly is compassionate he also judges us and we do not like being judged. Pilate felt this as Jesus stood before him as a prisoner wearing the crown of thorns and the purple robe. But who was judging whom? Who comes out of the trial scene as the condemned man? Is it not Pontius Pilate albeit sitting there as judge? Hear the scripture again. ' "Behold the Man!" said Pilate.' And then this: 'Take him and crucify him yourselves; for my part I find no case against him.'

Yes, the incarnate Christ is the revelation of man, what he could be, but at the crucifixion he becomes also the revelation of what we are and how we need saving from ourselves. So a revelation of the highest is not sufficient. We need action on the part of the incarnate Christ to give us the power to reconcile us to the revelation, in other words to be what we know we ought to be. And this power is in the crucified and risen Christ and in the coming of his Holy Spirit apprehended by faith in him. This is the gospel, the whole gospel, Christ not only as the revelation of what man could be, but Christ as the Saviour of what man is, frequently magnificent but more frequently flawed. '. . . and Jesus came out, wearing the crown of thorns and the purple cloak. "Behold the man!" ' We do well to behold him, the pattern man but also the Saviour – Jesus the incarnate Christ.

9

FOR OUR SALVATION

God was in Christ reconciling the world to himself.
2 CORINTHIANS 5.19 (NEB)

I begin with a statement. Jesus of Nazareth was a real man, not a man who looked like a man but in reality was not, Jesus was a real man. He certainly was not half-man and half-God, he was in every respect like as we are yet without sin. Jesus was a real man. We must never let this conviction go.

There are many people who would like to leave the matter there. In recent years, through plays, books and films, there has been something of a rediscovery of Jesus. His name is even seen on car stickers. The public imagination has to some extent been caught by him. No longer has he been counted as the preserve of the church stained-glass window, a stiff icon-like figure, scarcely real; Jesus was a man among men breathing as we breathe, enjoying company, caring for people whatever their background, respectable or not respectable, and not weak, on the contrary facing his opponents with cool bravery.

And more than this, at a deeper level, Jesus is counted a guide to living, a pioneer of faith, even a supreme revealer of God. He stands out from all others because he uniquely discovered God and lived out the full light of his discovery. What more then is required? Why complicate this exalted appreciation by calling him divine? Surely Jesus did not have to be God in order to reveal God! Is not the very notion of incarnation unnecessary?

1 THE GOD WHO SEEKS

There is however a question which will not go away – What kind of a God did he discover? Was he a God who waited to be discovered? Was he a passive deity whom a few unusually discerning and morally upright people succeeded in reaching? But was not the situation the complete reversal of this? Did not Jesus know and proclaim God as the Good Shepherd, one who not only cares for the sheep safely penned but actually goes in search of the lost and straying, notwithstanding whatever might have been the cause of their predicament, whether circumstances or their own grievous fault? And this was in line with the Hebrew scriptures which constituted the background of Jesus' religion. The story there is not of Abraham, Isaac and Jacob discovering God but of God discovering Abraham, Isaac and Jacob. And so with Moses, Gideon, Samuel, David, Isaiah, Jeremiah, to name but a few at random. The scriptures tell of God as the One who discovers men and women, not of One whom we first of all have to discover. This is the God whom Jesus revealed, the prevenient God, the God who goes in front, the God who takes the initiative. How then, I ask, could this God be adequately disclosed except by *coming himself* among us as a man, in other words the Incarnation, 'And the Word became flesh and dwelt among us'.

And so we see this incarnate God, this man Jesus, mixing with people at their level whatever it happened to be, publicans and sinners, Pharisee hosts at dinner tables, little children with their mothers crowding round, sick men and women, dirty people, unwashed and smelly. He did not draw back from the contagiously diseased, nor avoid the mentally deranged, nor the sightless and lame shuffling along. Wherever there were disadvantaged people at hand he met them. Take away the Incarnation, take away the faith that *God* was in Christ and you take away the great distinctive feature of the Christian Gospel, that indeed which makes it a Gospel, God seeking us before we begin to seek him. The initiative is with God.

2 GOD AND MAN

And now we move on. We have stressed the point that Jesus was a real man. Now we have to stress the point that he was also divine, he was God. And so our confession of Jesus is that he was God *and* man.

This is difficult. Of course it is difficult. How could a man walking about in Judaea and Galilee be God *and* man? Not surprisingly down the ages thinkers have wrestled with this problem, and answers, purporting to be explanations, have been suggested, none of them satisfactory. One idea was that Jesus as a man lived such a good life that God raised him to the status of divinity. But this gives man the priority in the salvation process, not God. Another idea was that God became man for a time, for about thirty years or more, that is, the life span of Jesus. But what was God doing for that thirty years? Yet another idea was that in the man Jesus, the Logos, or Word of God, replaced Jesus' human soul. But then Jesus would be neither truly God nor truly man. Discussion about all this raged (and raged is not too strong a word) for four hundred years or more in the early Church till it was decided at a great Council in Chalcedon in the year 451 that Jesus was truly God and truly man without mixing or truncating of either Godhead or manhood.

But that, you say, is no solution. We are no nearer to knowing *how* Jesus could be both God and man: and the objection is a real one. This however was the supreme merit of the Council of Chalcedon, it safeguarded the deity and the humanity of Jesus, maintaining that if either were watered down the Gospel of our Lord Jesus Christ would be lost. So the Creed in which this is enshrined is not meant to be a set of railings keeping us in a mental prison where we cannot even think our own thoughts, it is a balustrade, a hand-rail to help us reach a safe landing about what we believe about the person of Jesus. The Council of Chalcedon is a safeguard, no more, no less.

3 A PARADOX

Let us accept then that Jesus is God *and* man. What I wish to follow is the interpretation ably presented by a great Scottish theologian, that is of a paradox. Now a paradox is something which is seemingly absurd – two opposites unable to be coincided for each cancels out the other. But do they? Anyone who turns to page 1 of Ian MacLeod's *Preaching on the Lord's Supper* (1990) will find a drawing known as Kohler's Cross. Clearly it is a white cross on a black background, a Maltese Cross. But stare at it a little longer and you will see it is a black cross on a white background in the shape of St Andrew's cross. Now which is correct? Both are correct. So it is with Jesus. Looked at one way he is truly God. Looked at another way he is truly man. Both are correct. Jesus is God *and* man, a paradox.

Now paradox is at the very heart of the Christian life as we experience it. Any man or woman whose character and life-style approximates in any degree to that which must be called Christian will be the last person to claim 'By my own effort I am what I am'. No, they will say 'By the Grace of God I am what I am, but for God, heaven knows where I would be'. Yet at the same time they will know that they were not puppets on God's string. Their actions and struggles were really their own. Paradox then! Looked at one way we are what we are because of God's action. Looked at another way we are what we are because of our own actions. St Paul put it in a nutshell when he wrote to the Philippians, 'work out your own salvation . . . for it is God that works in you' (2.12). Or again 'by the grace of God I am what I am . . . but I laboured more abundantly than they all: yet not I, but the grace of God which was with me' (1 Corinthians 15.10 (AV)). There is paradox in the spiritual life of all of us which Harriet Auber perfectly captured in her hymn:

And every virtue we possess,
And every victory won,
And every thought of holiness,
Are his alone.

Is it surprising then that paradox should stand at the very base of the Christian proclamation, Jesus was God *and* man? This is what the Incarnation declares, a mystery, yes, but not a nonsense. It belongs to the supreme mystery of the Godhead which in essence is beyond us.

4 WHY DID GOD BECOME MAN?

There is still one major question to ask: why did God become man? Why the Incarnation at all? The Creed answers 'who for us men and for our salvation came down from heaven, And was incarnate by the Holy Ghost of the Virgin Mary', Don't feel trapped by the phrase 'came down from heaven'. This is symbolic language, and has nothing to do with space or the sky up there. Concentrate now on 'who for us men and for our salvation'. God became incarnate for our sakes, he became incarnate in order to save us, for we need saving. Unaided man makes a mess of this world.

But was there a need for anything more than a bare Incarnation? Could not Christmas stand by itself as the means of our salvation and the essence of the gospel? Why the life story of Jesus? why the Cross and Passion? Could we not be assured by the manger scene that God loves us? But what the taking of our human flesh did not, does not, by itself meet is the problem of human sinfulness.

It does not mediate forgiveness. It does not therefore reconcile us to God. So to remedy this situation God not only became incarnate, in Jesus he lived close in with sinners, never separating himself from them and becoming hated by those who counted themselves superior for doing so, but still he continued, he continued till his enemies brought him to the Cross. Jesus died because he would never forsake sinners, cast them off, nor repudiate them. In this way he carried their sins on his own back to the Cross showing there what the heart of God is always like, always has been, and always will be. God pays the price and forgives. The forgiveness is not there without the price. Forgiveness without suffering is immoral. It is a mere shrugging of the shoulders.

Why the Incarnation? Once more we ask the question. And the answer – to reconcile us to God. So St Paul in my text for this sermon: 'God was in Christ reconciling the world to himself, no longer holding men's misdeeds against them' (2 Corinthians 5.19 (NEB)). But be careful, we cannot crudely assert that God became incarnate in Jesus *in order that* he might be crucified and save us. This would make the life of Jesus artificial, even unnecessary. No, God became incarnate *and, as his life worked out*, showed all the while that God loves even sinners: and rather than go back on that love he would prefer to die if his enemies closed in on him, and they did close in, and he did die. No wonder that St Paul wrote to the Romans 'God commendeth his love toward us, in that, while we were yet sinners, Christ died for us' (Romans 5.8). And now there is nothing that brings men and women home to God as does the proclamation, the preaching of God in Christ reconciling the world to himself at the Cross of Calvary. Then we see why God became incarnate. We really do.

10

THE VICTORIOUS INCARNATE CHRIST

Bearing the human likeness, revealed in human shape, he humbled himself, and in obedience accepted even death – death on a cross. Therefore God raised him to the heights and bestowed on him the name above all names, that at the name of Jesus every knee should bow – in heaven, on earth, and in the depths – and every tongue confess, 'Jesus Christ is Lord', to the glory of God the Father.

PHILIPPIANS 2.7–11 (NEB)

I was struck the other day by the memory of a woman, an OAP, and long since dead, who was always cheerful. Right up to the age of eighty-seven, and with the aches and pains that normally come with advancing years, she continued to look on the bright side of life. It was no wonder she made friends with people of all ages, young as well as old. She could laugh, tell a funny story and yet sympathize with those less fortunate than herself, a rare combination.

We could wish the atmosphere in our churches always evidenced a similar brightness, and our worship too, not omitting the preaching! It would be wonderful if we could always be sent home from church laughing – or wouldn't it? Life isn't funny all the way. Some of it is deadly serious, and if we are to meet people where they are we must be ready to enter with them into the dark patches of life as well as the sunny ones. And this we have to remember, I have to remember, when preaching about the incarnate Christ; it has its solemn side as well as its bright side. It is to this we come now. 'Bearing the human likeness, revealed in human shape, he humbled himself, and in obedience accepted even death – death on a cross.' So wrote St Paul in a famous passage of his letter to the Christians of Philippi. Perhaps it was a quotation from an early Christian hymn.

1 FLAWED HUMANITY

I have said that the incarnation of Christ is a revelation of man, that is, of what men and women could be, because the Christ whom we worship lived in our human nature, or as St John put it 'the Word became flesh'. This is good to hear, we like it, and we are right to like it. We are reminded of what we know, that man is not essentially corrupt, men and women have enormous potentiality, enormous possibilities. Look at the astonishing array of saints that could be listed, men and women artists, scientists, writers, sculptors, painters, medical practitioners, quite apart from the thousands upon thousands of humble folk achieving noble lives against crippling odds.

The incarnation of Christ, however, does not only mean that God appeared in our promising human nature, it means he took upon himself mankind as it has unfortunately come to be, badly flawed, branded with all manner of sordidness, inhumanity, cruelty, alienation from God and besotted with bitter hatreds. To put it mildly, though it might be expressed fiercely, the story of the human race from the beginning until now is profoundly disappointing. This then, this marred mankind, is what Christ took for his own in the incarnation. It is for this that he became man, man's representative, thus identifying himself bodily with man's dismal record. No one has expressed this more bluntly than St Paul in his letter to the Corinthians (2 Corinthians 5.21 (RSV)): 'For our sake he [God] made him to be sin who knew no sin'.

If what I am saying is true, and I can but say that it is true to what the New Testament teaches, then we can begin to see a little why Christ on the cross uttered that terrible cry, 'My God, my God, why has thou forsaken me?' Not that his personal communion with God was severed, or there would have been no appeal to him at all, but he was embodying in himself humanity as it is, not as it might be. And nothing shows up its sorry state so devastatingly as that when God became incarnate to show his infinite care, cruelly he was killed for it. So he was thrust into the blackness of cosmic darkness by the awfulness of this evil intent, a darkness so thick that he felt it physically in his agony in the Garden of Gethsemane even before the cross was actually set up. It was a terror not primarily of nails being hammered into living flesh, many men and some women have endured more in the torture dungeons of Europe in this century, but a devilish terror – I use the adjective with care – compounded of the whole of humanity's age-long iniquity. I cannot explain this, I cannot begin to explain it, I even shrink from spelling it out in this bald fashion; I can only bare my head in the presence of the appalling mystery that somehow in the incarnation Christ embodied our sinful humanity. What is more, rather than not embody it, rather than let it be, festering in its continuity, he actually preferred death, oppressively public death at cruel hands with the consequent experience of impenetrable darkness. In short, the incarnation meant death for Jesus because of what we have made of our human nature, our flesh, which he assumed.

2 THE BREAKING OF HIS BODY

Let me bring this a little nearer home. Let me bring it into the sphere of our worship in church. In another sermon on another occasion I hope to say something about the incarnation and the sacrament of Holy Communion. At the moment I simply wish to direct your attention to what is technically called 'the fraction' in its administration. Before the priest distributes the bread he breaks it as Christ broke it at the Last Supper, he lets the communicants see him break it. It is always broken bread that we receive in the Eucharist.

Yes, it would be splendid to reflect how Christ took our human nature, yours and mine, in which to reveal that wonderful life of his in Galilee and Judaea. It would 'set us up no end', but the truth is it broke him and he was willing to be broken *for us*, he was obedient unto death, even death upon a cross.

The phrase 'for us' or 'on our behalf' is difficult. How can the death of Christ, the crucifixion of Christ be 'for us' or 'on our behalf'? We can appreciate, perhaps, how he became incarnate to show what man could be, and this is encouraging; we might even accept the cross as showing that God shares our pain and suffering. This is comforting. But what are we to make of Christ *dying* for us, Christ dying on our behalf? Does this mean that Christ is our substitute? a perfect sacrifice offered to propitiate an angry God at the mess we have made of life? But this would be immoral. I suggest – and I put it this way because various explanations have been offered – I suggest that what we see in Jesus on the cross is the completion of a life of absolute obedience to the will of God against all temptations, all odds, up to and including his death so that he could shout triumphantly with a loud voice from the cross itself 'It is finished'. So St John's gospel. The cross is the place of complete victory *in the place of apparent defeat.* In the life of Jesus, the incarnate Christ, sin did not win the deadly battle for the soul of man as to a greater or lesser degree it always does, in him sin was defeated. As we then unite ourselves in faith, by whatever means, to him we experience in ourselves to a greater or lesser degree his victorious life. Christ then died and completed the battle of his whole incarnate life *for us.* His victory stands for all time for us to share. We share it by putting ourselves on his side, and by calling ourselves his and meaning it. Describe this as saving faith in the crucified Christ, if you will, or any other phrase that will convey, however inadequately, this understanding.

3 THE CROWNING OF THE VICTOR

This has already been a long, and in a way, difficult sermon, but one more point must be added. The cross is the place of Christ's crowning. It is the battlefield where he won the battle of complete obedience to the will of God, the place where in this one man the back of sin in humanity was completely broken. It is therefore a true insight that has made artists in paint and stone depict the crucified Christ wearing on the cross not a crown of thorns but a golden crown, truly it is appropriate to employ such descriptive phrases as 'he reigns from the tree'. In the four gospels it is St John who brings out this truth about the crucified Jesus. The other three gospels present as it were a clear photograph of what actually happened on Good Friday, whereas St John gives us an interpretive portrait.

Let me then emphasize the point. The death of Christ is where the battle was fought and won for us. It was a place of blood, sweat, toil and tears. A cross therefore is the symbol proper to the Christian faith, a golden cross. The resurrection on Easter Day was what sealed that victory and began the ingathering of the fruits of it. His work completed, the risen Christ ascended to the throne of glory which was rightly his. Hear again the text with which we began our thinking today, 'bearing the human likeness, revealed in human shape, he humbled himself, and in obedience accepted even death – death on a cross. Therefore God raised him to the heights and bestowed on him the name above all names, that at the name of Jesus every knee should bow – in heaven, on earth, and in the depths – and every tongue confess, "Jesus Christ is Lord", to the glory of God the Father.' Surely this text says it all!

11

THE SOURCE OF ETERNAL LIFE

'Lord, to whom shall we go? Your words are words of eternal life.'

JOHN 6.68 (NEB)

Here is a congregation objecting to a sermon. No uncommon situation, you say; but some sermons are not worth objecting to, they are too dull; they wouldn't disturb a dog asleep on the pulpit ledge. But not this sermon. It got under the hearers' skin. And if they didn't shout out their protests – though I am not sure – their protests were evident by the way they wagged their heads, stared blankly at one another and shrugged their shoulders. And when the sermon was over, they stampeded for the exits leaving behind a sea of empty pews never to be filled again. But what is that tiny group by the exit which seems not to be sure what to do? First they appear to leave with the crowd, then to hang back, obviously they are in two minds. Who are they? And who was the preacher? And where did this take place? Let me tell you. The tiny hesitating group consisted of the twelve disciples, the preacher was none other than Christ himself, and the place was the Capernaum synagogue. What the congregation objected to was the message of the preacher, 'I am the bread of life'.

1 SURPRISING FREEDOM TO CHOOSE

Now when the building was empty Jesus addressed the tiny group of twelve hesitating men, his disciples. Clearly they were playing with the idea of deserting him too. What he said took them aback. 'Do you also want to leave me?' My guess is, if anything, they expected a sharp rebuke, 'Look, you are the chosen Twelve, appointed to be with me, to learn from me and to go out and work among men and women as my special representatives, apostles, "sent ones". You can't back out like these crowds. Stay here. I command you. Stick to your responsibilities!' But no command came. They knew how deeply he cared for them and depended on them, but all he said was 'Do you also want to leave me?' There was no compulsion, no pressure, not even moral pressure. He left them quite free to make their own choice. I guess they found it surprising.

Here is an up-to-date story of a patient brought into a public ward in a hospital late one evening, a casualty. He did not know what was the nature of his trouble, but the surgeon soon arrived to examine him, and this is the conversation that ensued. Strong protests on the part of the patient because the surgeon intimated that he would be required to stay in bed a few days. 'But I can't' was the objection sharply uttered. 'I am a busy man, I have work to do this week, I run a business. I must leave in the morning, and I will. Give me some medicine, and I will be all right.' And this is how the surgeon replied. 'Of course', he said, 'you can leave first thing in the morning. This is a free country. You are a free man. You can do just as you like, but my advice to you is to stay where you are and do as I tell you.' And he strode out of the ward. Next morning, the patient was still there, as he was for most of the following week till he went home cured.

Christ put no pressure on his disciples to stay with him. And if you believe in the Incarnation as I do, if you believe that God was in Christ in all that he did and said, you will see how God puts no pressure on us to believe in him, or to stay with him or to do what he says. We are all free to disbelieve in God if we so will and to break all the commandments. God will employ neither pleasure nor pain, neither success in life nor failure to *drive* us into his arms. God is no tyrant, no dictator, no slave driver. He has authority as Jesus had authority, absolute authority. People sensed it almost as soon as they saw him; but his authority was not force, it was rooted in such a concern for people's welfare that only one word seems fitting to describe it, the authority of love. When we look at the incarnate Christ we are looking at the very nature of God.

2 THE DANGER OF RELATIVISM

And now a second observation. Come back to the twelve disciples at the synagogue exit hesitating. When Jesus asked if they were also quitting Peter spoke up, 'Lord, to whom shall we go? Your words are words of eternal life.' Shall we be right if we count this as Peter's personal response to the preaching of Jesus which gave such offence to the congregation, and which said in effect, 'I am the bread of life'? I think so. Peter was confessing, there is no other hold for us to make but you when it comes to obtaining eternal life.

It is precisely here that we are in trouble today. We haven't anything on which to take hold. We do not recognize any absolute values. We have no stable standards of conduct. Everything is relative. Granted it was not the aim of Einstein's theory of relativity propounded at the beginning of this century, nevertheless the result has been to make everything relative, not least in the realm of morals. Absolute standards are obsolete which, in popular thought, means that what is right or wrong is a matter of individual opinion, and yours is as good as mine. What is more, conduct is relative to time, circumstances and cultural conditioning. No one can declare what ought always to be done, and ought always to be approved, and so morally we are at sea. And the confusion has been compounded by the popularizing of Freud's psychological theories by which no one can be held to be responsible personally for his actions, we are all conditioned by our genes and by our involvement in the whole human race. And so, of course, the concept of sin is outmoded, and certainly of guilt with the accompanying call to repentance. These ideas have influenced some Biblical studies so that, for example, St Paul's condemnation of certain sexual practices is not worth serious consideration as regulating modern behaviour for he was culturally conditioned by the age in which he lived. Everything is relative. There are no absolute standards.

Now it must be admitted that no one except the very young or very foolish will reckon that life can easily be divided into black and white. Ours is a grey world and our experience of it is grey. If however there can be no marker buoys at all in the sea of life by means of which we can confidently steer our course, but everything is relative, we need not be surprised if ordinary people feel utterly lost. A vivid picture of this sort of confusion comes to my memory when I recall my boyhood and 'teenage' years spent on the Norfolk coast within sight of treacherous sandbanks some five or six miles offshore visible only at very low tides. A busy shipping lane passed between the sandbanks and the shore. No vessel, however, would have dared to use that channel without the string of buoys lit up at night and fitted with fog-horns for misty conditions. For safe travel fixed guides are essential.

Is this the principle Peter had grasped when with his fellow disciples he was tempted to cut loose from Jesus because of his occasional 'hard sayings', 'Lord, to whom shall we go? Your words are words of eternal life.' If we lose you, Lord, we shall drift in a sea of uncertainty. You are the light of the world. You are the bread of life. And so he stayed with Christ and his example caused his fellow disciples to stay as well. A bold example can have this salutary effect. No, *Christ* is not relative. He is *the light* by whom we are invited to let our way be guided.

3 EVANGELISM

And now a third consideration. It concerns evangelism, much to the fore in the Church's thinking in the 1990s. What should be the essence of this evangelistic effort? I believe it should be the proclamation of the incarnate Christ as our fixed guide and our saviour. Notice how broadly I have phrased this but also how definitely. It is not too much to say that we in Britain today are floundering in a sea of meaninglessness. We do not know what life is about. We do not know how to handle ourselves or the environment. We do not know what is our destiny. We are mere cogs in a wheel over which we have no control. In this semi-darkness the Christian Gospel makes a bold, some would say, a naive proclamation. Christ is the true light, in shutting our eyes to whom we lose our way. Light is the first necessity for salvation from disaster in any kind of journey and certainly for the passage from the cradle to the grave, a permanent, unflickering light. Christ is that light and evangelism is drawing people's eyes towards him.

Some people, even some Christian people are afraid of this word evangelism. I am not surprised if it is conceived in terms of emotional manipulation of large audiences, or for that matter of individuals. Of these high-pressure tactics we have seen examples in America and not only in America. I would have you notice that this was not Christ's way. He put no pressure even on the twelve apostles to stay with him. 'Do you also want to leave me?' was all he said when they hesitated. When a rich young ruler could not face up to the demands placed upon him to renounce his possessions but walked away Jesus watched him go sadly for he loved the man, but he did not run after him, he let him go. When on that cross of wood on Good Friday, one thief impaled next to him repented, and the one on the other side did not, Jesus put no pressure on the unrepentant one to change his mind. Both thieves had the same Christ next to them, both heard the words to the one, 'Today you will be with me in paradise', that was preaching enough. Jesus turned no screw. He left the matter there.

The scripture passage from St John, chapter 6, we have been considering today reminds us that evangelism consists primarily in helping people to see Christ clearly, by deeds as well as by words, and then leaving them free to make their response as Peter made his, 'Lord, to whom shall we go? Your words are words of eternal life.' God does not manipulate us. Christ did not manipulate anyone. Our hearers and observers certainly must be left in no doubt what is our message, the Incarnate Christ, Son of God, son of man, who lived and died and rose again for us. In him is our eternal life, but we are left to make our own response of 'yes' or 'no'. This is the heart of evangelism. It does involve a decision. We make it of course when we receive the bread and the wine in the Eucharist. Let us see that it does not become mechanical.

12

BELIEVING IS SEEING

So he went and washed and came back seeing.

JOHN 9.7 (RSV)

Today I am going to tell you a story, not my story but a story from St John's gospel. I make no apology for this. Because the Word was made flesh, and the incarnate Christ dwelt among us, we must expect to read of him in our world, acting and reacting to a variety of circumstances. So time and again, St John breaks away from spiritual profundities to tell stories, plain and simple, well, plain, anyway. One such is in chapter 9 about a blind man. This is what I am going to open up. It is really about seeing, believing and light, but not in the form of abstract statements, instead about a man who could not see.

1 HEALING NOT SPECULATION

Jesus came across him by chance and stopped to look at him. My guess is the man bore a notice attached to his person sufficiently large and legible for the most casual passer-by to read. It said 'Blind from birth', and beside him of course the inevitable begging bowl. Doorways to religious buildings – and this incident took place close by the Jerusalem Temple – have always been favourite places for beggars to squat. They reckoned the religious would hope to gain eternal merit by relieving the miseries of the poor. It was a hope that suited the poor. It paid into their collecting bowls.

As St John has arranged his gospel this story follows directly on an account of a nasty incident in the Temple precincts. The Jews, incensed by Jesus' teaching, picked up stones to fling at him. It was the kind of scene captured for us today by the television cameras covering hostilities between Jews and Arabs in the Gaza Strip, ugly scenes. Jesus was forced to take cover, and that quickly, perhaps he ran. Anyway he made a getaway. I don't know if St John intends us to understand that this was the occasion when something about this blind beggar caused him to stop and regard him, if so his coolness in the wake of a hot situation was remarkable. This much is certain; the setting of this story is one of extreme tension. There were people in and around the Temple who would stop at nothing.

Jesus paused to regard this blind man, some disciples with him. They paused when they saw him pause. They looked to see what he saw. Then they asked a silly question. 'Rabbi, who sinned, this man or his parents, that he was born blind?' It was a silly question on two accounts. Blindness or any other disability is not necessarily the consequence of the sufferer's sin. This nevertheless was current thought and the disciples had fallen for it. It was also a silly question because the man was *born* blind. How then could his blindness be the consequence of his sin? But could the cause be some sin on the part of the parents? Diseases can be transmitted from parent to child, contracted in the first place by misbehaviour. So perhaps the disciples' question was not so silly after all. Jesus however swept all this aside. He was not concerned with attributing blame, only with healing. Listen to his words. 'It was not that this man sinned, or his parents but that the works of God might be made manifest in him.' 'As he said this, he spat on the ground and made clay of the spittle and anointed the man's eyes with the clay, saying to him, "Go, wash in the pool of Siloam" (which means Sent). So he went and washed and came back seeing.'

2 MORE QUESTIONS

We can be sure he looked different. A seeing man has a different look about his face from an unseeing one. Doubt can even arise about his identity. Is he really the same man? Note this. We shall come back to it in a minute. Meanwhile imagine how the cured blind man walked, he no longer shuffled. Everything around him was new, novel and mysterious. He stared.

Did, I wonder, one of the disciples nudge another and whisper, 'I say, John, I say, Peter; what is that bit in the Bible, "Then shall the eyes of the blind be opened and the ears of the deaf be unstopped, then shall the lame man leap as an hart and the tongue of the dumb shall sing"? Doesn't this relate to the time of Messiah when he comes? But surely, that cannot be the Messiah standing over there, he who has just spat on the ground, made clay of the spittle and anointed the eyes of that blind man! But he can see! the blind man can see! his eyes have been opened!' And so it was that Jesus puzzled all those who watched him, even his disciples. Who was he? The idea of God incarnate was utterly foreign to them, as indeed it is for many people today.

In passing we cannot help asking why Jesus spat on the ground, made clay of the spittle and anointed the eyes of the blind man? Would not the clay seal up his eyes rather than open them? And why not cure with a word? He had done so before. Why use a medium for healing? and such a messy medium, though one according to the elementary medical notions of the time possessed of healing properties. And why send the blind man to the pool of Siloam to wash in waters supposed to be curative? Was all this done to arouse expectancy in the man? or was it simply in line with the whole principle of the Incarnation to use material means and physical actions to convey the power of the spiritual?, and also to come down to people's level? We do well to ask these questions, even if we cannot know the answers. We must remain content with a picture of a man blind from birth seeing the light of day for the first time. That light meant new life for him, and all through the action of the incarnate Christ.

3 THE DARKNESS OF HOSTILITY

But the scene changes. Clouds and darkness cover the sky. All around were men waiting to destroy this healer. The stoning in the Temple area had failed. Jesus had made his 'getaway'. Here then was a chance to trap him with the law, better than employing mob violence. The Jewish law expressly forbad anointing eyes with clay on the Sabbath and Jesus had done just this. So the cured blind man could be used as a tool with which to incriminate Jesus. Here we see religion at its worst. Ceremonial rubrics taking precedence over people. Did Jesus then, for his part, deliberately choose this method of healing because it was forbidden by the religious law in order to explode it? Be that as it may, the man was caught and a clear statement extracted from him as to the means by which he could now see.

His testimony was firm, he could not be shaken from it, not even when his parents were brought and declared that he was indeed their son and that he had been born blind. But explanations or even suggestions as to how he was able to see could not be dragged from them. They feared excommunication. A second time therefore the cured man was brought before the tribunal but to no avail, he not only stuck to his testimony, he dared to taunt his judges. After all he had nothing to lose. So the authorities' ploy was a flop. Furious, they threw the erstwhile beggar out. He had nowhere to go. We can picture him wandering the streets.

4 THE CLIMAX

So we reach the final paragraph of the story. Jesus found this lost man. The wording suggests a search. Did he re-visit the Temple site where he first encountered him as a beggar with his placard and begging bowl? Did he scour the vicinity of the Pool of Siloam? No one helped. All he could learn was that the man had been thrown out. But Jesus found him. We ought to let this event and its meaning sink into our consciousness. It is in the hope of this that the story is told. God seeks us when we are in need. 'The Son of man came to seek and to save that which was lost.' And the wry thought is that this one was lost in the religious capital of the world! What a story! But let us not miss the point. Here we see the divine initiative at work. This is the incarnate Christ. God finds us before we find him.

Now the grand climax, the God–man encounter. Jesus addressed the now seeing man, 'Do you believe in the Son of man?' Believing is connected with seeing. He didn't know who he was. Like many in our twentieth century, he had vague ideas – a prophet possibly, someone 'from God' maybe. Then Jesus disclosed himself and the joyous response was elicited, 'Lord I believe'. Nor was this all, he worshipped him, the worship of the incarnate Christ was the index of genuine faith. He had indeed seen the light.

And so the story has come all the way from Christ being stoned to Christ being worshipped. At one end hostility, at the other end faith. Who then were the blind? Were they not the ones picking up stones in the Temple area to fling at Jesus? And why did the man born blind come to the experience of seeing? Because he believed Jesus' command and obeyed, 'Go wash in Siloam'. He could see because he believed. Believing is seeing. Hear the text again – John 9.7: 'So he went and washed and came back seeing.'

Thus the darkness of this man's life was pierced. Light shone all around him. He experienced another world. And he looked different, so different, people questioned his identity. A living faith does change people, yes today. They see around them with different eyes and they themselves are seen in a different light. Contemporary stories on this are legion. Thumb back to the opening verses of St John's gospel. Did we grasp their meaning? Of the incarnate Logos the Christ they read: 'In him was life; and the life was the light of men. The light shone in the darkness and the darkness has not overcome it.' We needed a simple illustration in story form. Apparently St John thought so, which is why he wrote in chapter 9 about a nameless blind man who at Jesus' command 'went and washed and came back seeing'.

13

THE LIGHT OF LIFE

'I am the resurrection and the life; he who believes in me, though he die, yet shall he live, and whoever lives and believes in me shall never die.'

JOHN 11.25, 26 (RSV)

I have to tell another story from St John's gospel. I can't help myself. Having been bitten with the story of the restoration to sight of the man born blind, I am unable to leave standing the story of Lazarus raised to life, because the two are connected. They disentangle the twin themes of light and life introduced in the opening of the gospel, 'In him [the incarnate Christ] was life and the life was the light of men'. The blind man received the light of his eyes; Lazarus, the sick, dead and buried man, received life from the grave. Both situations were accounted hopeless, and both were said to be reversed for the glory of God. If I have told the one story, I have to tell the other. Here it is.

1 A HOUSE OF DARKNESS

First we have to visualize a house in a village called Bethany two miles outside Jerusalem. Not a rich house, I think, nor a poor house, which drives me to suggest (at some risk) a kind of middle-class house. Two sisters lived there with their brother, Lazarus. They were hospitable. They entertained Jesus and he felt at home there. This house may have been where he stayed during the last week of his life, thus avoiding the danger of residence in Jerusalem where men lurked bent on killing him. A close bond of affection existed between Jesus and these three people. Of Lazarus we know nothing apart from this one incident. Of the two women we have consistent pictures of their contrasting natures. Martha, the kind you would invite to run the village social; Mary the sort you would expect to find comforting some neighbour crushed by a personal calamity. Both had deep feelings but expressed them differently, Martha in bustling activity, Mary in quiet emotional involvement.

Of the two women Martha 'got more done', as we say, while Mary was deeper in understanding. Both were followers of Jesus, close followers, and he loved them both along with Lazarus, the brother. What is more, the family was a respected one in the community where they lived.

Suddenly calamity overtook them. No one is proof against the possibility of this, not even devoted followers of Jesus. Lazarus fell critically ill, and to crown all, just when Jesus, to whom the two women would instinctively turn, was miles away. He had gone to the other side of the Jordan river in order to be sufficiently free from the harassment of the Jerusalem authorities to teach his disciples unmolested. That Martha and Mary, unlike most people, knew his whereabouts is an index of their intimacy with him. They sent a message, 'Sir, [note the respect in which they held him] you should know that your friend lies ill' (NEB). Note also that they did not presume to tell him what to do, much less to return to help them; two reminders perhaps for our praying. Warmth of devotion should not cancel out reverence, and nor is praying telling God what to do. It is only mentioning need in his presence. Then this. Jesus stayed away a further two days. He did not respond immediately. And Lazarus died.

And so in this story we have a picture of a kind of darkness. There is no light because there is no life. It is different from the darkness of the man born blind. Two women groping in the bewildering darkness of bereavement, the absence of their closest friend and his puzzling silence when they send him a message. Now the shutters are up in the house, talking is reduced to a whisper and the steady procession of callers come to offer their condolences, the price of the respect in which they were held. And over and over again the two sisters repeating to each other, 'If only he [Jesus] had been here our brother would not have died'. It is a sad picture of two women clinging to each other in their grief.

2 ETERNAL LIFE NOW

At last a message. He, Jesus, is on the way. Martha, ever ready for action, could not wait. She hurried to meet him as he approached the village. 'Sir', she cried, 'if you had been here my brother would not have died.' Was there a reproof in this? Martha could reprove. Did she then correct herself? 'Even now I know that whatever you ask of God, God will grant you.' Sidestepping this he said, 'Your brother will rise again'. And so the grand theme of this story comes into view, resurrection and life, especially life. It was orthodox doctrine that there would be resurrection at the last day. Martha believed the doctrine and said so to Jesus. He believed it too, but there was more to be added, much more. Acceptance of an established doctrine is not the heart of faith. This only comes by way of personal trust in a God who acts personally, a way which stood wide open for Martha with the incarnate Christ facing her on the roadway outside her village of Bethany. He said, 'I am the resurrection and the life; he who believes in me, though he die, yet shall he live, and whoever lives and believes in me shall never die'. Did her eyes reveal a flicker of doubt? After all Martha was Martha. So he pressed her very gently, 'Do you believe this?' And there came forth the majestic confession, 'I do. I now believe you are the Messiah, the Son of God who was to come into the world.'

And so the dimension of death was minimized, *is minimized*. In union with the incarnate Christ death cannot be other than temporary, a passing event, for he is *life*. Or as the prologue to St John's gospel has it (1.4, 5), 'In him was life, and the life was the light of men. The light shines in the darkness, and the darkness has not overcome it.' Let us be clear on this. Immortality is not a human attribute, it is a divine attribute, but it can be ours through faith, union with him, and that union is made easy by the incarnate Christ come to our world. Martha stood face to face with this stupendous reality on the roadway outside her village of Bethany brought sharply into focus when he said, 'Do you believe this?' Faith realizes the gift of eternal life now. Preaching the incarnate Christ brings this assurance.

3 THE JUSTIFICATION FOR GRIEF

So what about grief in the face of bereavement? Are tears, mourning and heart-breaking sorrow out of place in the light of the eternal life which is ours through faith in Christ? We continue with the story for answer.

Jesus asked to see Mary. The request made to Martha propelled her in haste to convey the news. She knew only too well where Mary would be, back in the darkened house crushed by the bereavement that had overtaken her. Martha's message was electric. In an instant it lifted her up. 'The Master is here and is asking for you.' Did she run? Who can doubt it? Her sudden movement however puzzled the attendant mourners for they were not privy to Martha's message. They thought that maybe a paroxysm of grief was driving her to the brother's tomb. But they were wrong. It was Jesus outside the village drawing her with that all but incredible wish to see her. And as soon as she caught sight of him, true to her nature, and unlike her sister, she fell at his feet crying out the words she and Martha had uttered to each other a thousand times, 'O, Sir, if you had been here, my brother would not have died'.

Now with all the delicacy of feeling of which we are capable let us note the sequence. Jesus looked down at this woman crying her heart out. He would have had to be made of stone not to be deeply moved by the sight of her, and he wasn't made of stone. God is not made of stone. St John wrote that he sighed heavily and was deeply moved. In whatever way we translate the Greek words here we are driven to ask, Did he tremble? Was he perhaps incensed to see a woman like Mary beaten down by the enemy called death? Tenderly, we may be sure, he enquired, 'Where have you laid him?' The bystanders answered for her, 'Come and see, Sir'. And when they turned to look at him tears were streaming down his face.

Do we need any other answer to the question as to whether grief is inappropriate in the light of the Gospel that death is swallowed up in victory? Christian faith does not dehumanize people, it does not turn them into unfeeling dogmatists. Quite the reverse. Yes, there is a difference. Through our tears we see the incarnate Christ standing there crying with us, crying because we are crying, but also standing there as the One who will bring us to the place where all tears will be wiped away and there will be no more sighing, no more crying, nor any more pain.

Turn your head now to view the bystanders. They could not take their eyes off Jesus. Some commented, 'How dearly he must have loved him'. Others looked back to that extraordinary cure of the man born blind with which this story is linked and asked 'Could not this man who opened the blind man's eyes have done something to keep Lazarus from dying?'

4 THE CHALLENGING CLIMAX

And now the climax. I warn you. I warn myself. It takes some believing. But we shall not be asked to see any more signs like this. This is the seventh and last in St John's gospel except the resurrection of Christ himself. Jesus sighed deeply as he went over to the tomb. Was there an all but overwhelming struggle in him as he stretched forth to exercise the astounding power soon to be manifest? 'Take away the stone', he called. Martha was horrified. She feared the consequent exhibition of her beloved brother's decomposing corpse for he had been dead four days. But he countered her, 'Did not I tell you that if you have faith you will see the glory of God?' At once he prayed a prayer of thanksgiving that his Father had heard his prayer. Then he raised his voice in a great cry, 'Lazarus come forth', or in Greek, 'Lazarus, hither outside'. But Lazarus did not walk out. He couldn't. His feet and hands were bound in linen bands and his face wrapped in a cloth. Jesus himself would be wound round with grave clothes in the borrowed tomb of Joseph of Arimathea, but he, unlike Lazarus, burst the bonds of his death. Lazarus did not. Jesus called 'Loose him, and let him go'.

It is not for us to concern ourselves now with the reactions to this event, how some came to faith in the incarnate Christ because of what was done that day, and how others went off to report to the authorities the danger to the government of the country if a man with such powers as Jesus apparently possessed was left at large. What we need to grasp is how the story of Lazarus is set in St John's gospel as a vivid illustration of the two verses in the Prologue which read 'In him [the incarnate Christ] was life, and the life was the light of men. The light shines in the darkness, and the darkness has not overcome it' (1.4, 5).

There is nothing else to say. We can either let the story quicken our faith in the incarnate Christ in whom is light and life; or we can reject the suggestion as unworthy of intelligent consideration. We are free to pursue either course. There is no compulsion. Light does not compel, but it does show the way.

14

THE JUDGE AND THE SAVIOUR

For God sent not his Son into the world to judge the world; but that the world should be saved through him.

JOHN 3.17 (RV)

Some time ago a man I knew well remarked to me about a certain priest with whom we were both acquainted, 'You know, he is such a Christlike person'. I must confess this left me standing, not because I doubted in any way the excellence of the priest we had in mind, but because I wasn't sure what picture this description conjured up. In any case any comment I might venture would sound trite if not downright stupid, rather like saying that Rembrandt's painting of his mother in the Mauritshuis at The Hague is 'rather nice'. But on my way home I thought about this description 'Christlike'. I realized that this was the highest tribute that could be paid to this particular priest, he was 'Christlike'. He might be a good scholar, a competent organizer, an arresting preacher, a diligent parish visitor; perhaps he did possess one of more of these gifts and accomplishments; but any one of them, or all of them together, paled beside this one comment, 'You know, he is such a Christlike person'.

1 THE ULTIMATE MEASURE OF EXCELLENCE

And so there was underlined for me what I half knew that Christ is the ultimate index of what personal excellence is, the index of what goodness is, even what Godlikeness is. Christ is the ultimate measure, standard and criterion. There is nothing you can put in his place, and in this sense he is the final judge of us all, and of all human character. This of course must mean the *incarnate* Christ. You cannot have a rule without visible markings on it. You cannot measure any person or any action against a Christ who is no more than a bare name or a symbol for divinity. It is necessary to know what he said, what he did, and what manner of man he was. This places the historical Jesus in the forefront of our quest, not even to be displaced by the risen Christ.

Now I am rather tired of saying this, but I must get it out of the way and repeat it again before going any further, 'Christlike man' does not mean weakness. 'Gentle Jesus, meek and mild' is not the incarnate Christ we see in the gospels. No one ever felt they wanted to put their arms around him and protect him or comfort him. Only once was an attempt made to encourage him. This was by the impetuous apostle Peter on the day when Jesus began to speak of what he would suffer at Jerusalem and how he would be killed. Peter blurted out, 'God forbid, Lord. This shall never happen to you.' As much as to say, 'Cheer up, Lord, everything will be all right'. He was rebuked in no uncertain terms and classed as one not on God's side but on man's side. And when the mother of Jesus, no doubt counting on her special relationship, attempted on two occasions to interfere in his ministry she was firmly put down. Jesus was a compassionate man but he stood apart. Instinctively people called him 'Sir'. Typically, an army captain and, on another occasion, an official addressed him in this way. He gave the impression of expecting to be obeyed. He was not to be pushed around or cornered in argument, and never was he loquacious. If you read through St John's gospel you will see a man constantly engaged in confrontation and sometimes even provoking it. And should you object that his followers would not (would they now?) record any failures or even 'blips' on his part, I have to come back at you and reply, 'But you must admit that he consistently gave the impression of being a strong man or what has been written of him would never have been written'. The human Jesus was a long way from 'gentle Jesus meek and mild'. I have to stress this, otherwise there simply is no sense in describing Jesus as the ultimate index of excellence and the final judge of all human achievement.

2 AN IMMEASURABLE MEASURE

What then after all is Christlikeness? How is it to be described? The answer is, You can't do it. If you try you will only succeed in breaking it down into facets, and if you then concentrate on one facet, perhaps one that appeals to you, you will disturb the whole. All of which means that there is no alternative but to gaze, yes I said gaze, at the complete series of pictures of the incarnate Christ presented in the gospels; and to meditate upon them, even for a lifetime, then maybe we shall have some idea of what Christlikeness is. This too, must be added, each picture will impart something to us of his extraordinary stature and his difference from all of us. This is the startling fact, the incarnate Christ is God with us, God among us; that this should be so is the point of the incarnation, but he is still beyond us, still 'out there'; he is one of us, but he is also not one of us. This is the paradox of Jesus. Let me dare to express this in a brash fashion, We can never 'tape' Jesus.

Last winter we experienced some extremely rough weather. The winds blasted in from the Atlantic, trees bent to breaking point, slates clattered down from roofs, rain mixed with snow rendered roads dangerous to use. The North Sea, I was told, was frightening, and I could imagine it, having lived the first twenty years of my life within two hundred yards of the shore, witnessing more than one shipwreck. Then one afternoon in January the wind dropped and everything lay still. I ventured into my garden to clear up some of the mess that lay all around when, quite unexpectedly, the clouds lifted in the west leaving only little wisps and ripples here and there against a background of an azure sky. The time was about 3:30 and the sun began to set. I stood transfixed. The sight was ineffable. A delicacy of blue, pink and white comprising the dome of the heavens, lit up like an immense translucent painting. I have spent a lifetime juggling with words, spoken and written but before that scene of breathtaking beauty which lasted not more than seven minutes, I could only mutter, 'O you should have seen it'. I was struck dumb for words.

Not infrequently, perhaps more often than not, our reading or hearing of the gospel narratives stirs us little more than a cloud-packed sky. Then once in a while, and quite unexpectedly we see Him, we see Jesus the incarnate Christ. Probably it is too much to comment that our breath is taken away but we are left with nothing to say. We have glimpsed the ultimate of goodness. Was our experience a revelation? a revelation of the revelation which is Christ. There is a verse in the last book of the Old Testament which for its sheer beauty of expression catches at this truth, 'But for you who fear my name, the sun of righteousness shall rise with healing in his wings'.

3 REFLECTED GLORY

And now the amazing corollary, the glory of the incarnate Christ gets reflected in people we encounter so that we exclaim, 'O what a Christlike person!' There we have to stop as I stopped on that winter afternoon in my garden, transfixed by the glory of that multicoloured sky. When I turned to look at my house all the windows were shining too by reason of the reflection, and not only the windows of my house but the windows too of that large house in the park, and the cracked panes of glass in that tumbledown greenhouse along the road, and that old shed whose windows have not been cleaned except by the rain for years, even those bits of broken glass on the roadway, the result of a car accident, they twinkled in the brightness of the over-arching light.

This is the point. Whenever that brightness, wherever that light was seen, in whatever place, even unlikely place, and in whatever condition, it was *reflected* light that shone, not the light of the glass itself. Is this how we may experience sheer goodness in the world, perhaps in other cultures, other races, other religions, yes and in Christianity too? It is reflected light we see, reflected divine light, the true light of God, the light of the incarnate Christ. This is why we must respect those different interpretations of life however foreign to our own. There is no complete blackout anywhere. St John testifies to this in his gospel (1.5). 'The light shines in the darkness, and the darkness has not overcome it.'

So now we know what goodness is, sheer goodness. Whatever squares with the picture we have of the incarnate Christ as we have it in the gospels, that is goodness. Goodness is Christlikeness. It is the ultimate standard.

Some time ago Donald Nicholl wrote up this story in a book called *Holiness*. It is about a Buddhist hermit and teacher called Hakuin. One day a well-to-do young woman in a neighbouring fishing village, finding herself pregnant, declared that for all his far-famed holiness the hermit was in fact responsible for her condition. She stirred up her relatives who in a body trooped up the mountain where he lived in a hut to accuse him of what they said he had done to the girl, and to mock. He listened. He listened carefully and then he said 'Is that so?' This is all he said. When the child was born, whom no one wanted, Hakuin took it into his hut, nursed it and fondled it as if it were his own. A year and a half later, the child's mother, overcome with guilt, confessed that a local young fisherman was in fact the father of the child. Once again the relatives in a body trooped up to the hermit's hut in order to make protestations of their sorrow for having damaged the teacher's reputation for goodness. They said they realized that he was not the father of the child. 'Is that so?' were his only words by way of reply.

How else can this Buddhist's behaviour be described except as Christlike? Does not this text from the first epistle of St Peter in the New Testament (2.23) fit? It says Christ 'when he was reviled, reviled not again'. So I dare to repeat, the incarnate Christ is the measure of sheer goodness wherever it is found.

Is this a comfort? It is only partly a comfort, and for this reason, we are conscious of how far short we all fall from it. So the incarnate Christ is our judge. He is indeed the judge of all men and women. Standing up in the Areopagus in Athens St Paul put this plainly 'he [God] will judge the world in righteousness by that man whom he hath ordained; whereof he hath given assurance unto all men, in that he hath raised him from the dead' (Acts 17.31). He is not the judge in the sense of a condemning figure in the court room but as the one against whose goodness we are measured. Yes, we fail, all of us, fail miserably, but God is a God of infinite compassion, this too we see clearly in the incarnate Christ; he did not turn his back on sinners. All this is set out by St John in those striking verses in chapter 3 of his gospel, following on the Nicodemus story. 'For God sent not his Son into the world to judge the world; but that the world should be saved through him' – the text with which I began this sermon. Christlikeness is the standard against which we show up badly but it also tells of the infinite love of God. Christ is indeed our judge, but he is also our Saviour. 'For God so loved the world, that he gave his only begotten Son [the incarnate Christ], that whosoever believeth in him should not perish, but have everlasting life' (John 3.16).

15

RESURRECTION AND INCARNATION

For unto you is born this day in the city of David a Saviour, who is Christ the Lord.

LUKE 2.11 (AV)

So wrote St Luke in his gospel. So the announcement of the angel to the shepherds keeping watch over their flocks by night. We know the story. They hurried to Bethlehem and found Joseph and Mary, and the babe lying in a manger. Did they think, I wonder, that they were looking at a saviour when they saw the baby? He did not look like a saviour or a deliverer, but does any baby? Nor did the circumstances of his cradling suggest any kind of saviour to come; but then, more than one national leader in the long story of mankind has arisen from humble circumstances. What about Moses, the founder of the Israelite nation? Did he look like the deliverer of his people from the slave camps of Egypt when he lay in the basket of bulrushes his mother had prepared for him and floated him on the waters of the Nile where by the edict of the Pharaoh he was supposed to be drowned?

1 AN ARRESTING PERSON

About Jesus I go further. Did he look like a saviour when he was planing wood in his carpenter's shop at Nazareth and repairing his neighbours' furniture or farm implements? And later still, did he look like a saviour when he was preaching in the synagogues of Galilee, and opening the eyes of the blind, and unstopping the ears of the deaf and cleansing the lepers? Certainly people must have counted him an extraordinary man gifted with extraordinary powers, but a saviour? This was hard to believe with Roman soldiers stationed at every vantage point throughout the land to keep the Jews in subjection. And if there were any grand ideas of him as a saviour, and once or twice they did bubble up, they were utterly shattered when they saw him crucified between two terrorists like any common criminal.

Am I being difficult? I am saying all this in order to drive home this point that whatever intuition a few men and women might have had about Jesus during his lifetime on earth, no one with him then thought of him as God incarnate. Yes, he was a wonderful man, a miracle worker, an outstanding preacher and a wisdom teacher, a prophet, even a man indwelt by God, that is by the Spirit of God, perhaps a man who might even restore the Kingdom of Israel; who could tell? But God incarnate? No. This did not enter their thinking. And it never would have entered anyone's thinking had not something stupendous happened which was the resurrection of the crucified Jesus from the dead on Easter Day. So this is the point I am at pains to make. We believe in the Incarnation because we believe in the Resurrection; or we do not believe in the Incarnation because we do not believe in the Resurrection. The Incarnation and the Resurrection of Christ stand or fall together, and we begin with the Resurrection not the Incarnation. This is the place to start if we would grasp who Jesus is.

2 PROGRESSIVE UNDERSTANDING

And now a second point. A long time elapsed before the Christian Church reached an accepted conclusion about Christ and who he really was and is. That elaborate definition in the Nicene Creed we recite in our Eucharistic worship – 'God of God, Light of Light, Very God of very God, Begotten, not made . . .' – took some four hundred years to settle; even so what it really worked out was only a settlement of the boundaries of our thinking about Christ beyond which to stray would be unwise if we wish to preserve our faith. None of this, of course, was in the apostle Peter's mind when he stood up to preach in Jerusalem on the Day of Pentecost. His thinking had indeed been opened up concerning Jesus by the resurrection on Easter Day but his message was simple, 'God has made this Jesus whom you crucified both Lord and Christ'. And preaching to Cornelius and his friends at Caesarea he described Jesus as one 'who went about doing good and healing all that were oppressed by the devil, for God was with him'.

I am anxious to point out these statements illustrating the straightforward, even simple, understanding which even the leading apostles had at first of the Person of Christ because they may save from despair any today, perhaps here in Church, who may be 'put off' by abstract credal statements, 'put off' even by words like 'incarnation', which, by the way, does not occur anywhere in the New Testament. I am anxious that the gospel shall not be blurred which declares that we are safe (some might want to say 'saved') by believing in Jesus who died and rose again. So he is our Lord. On this bedrock of faith we may rightly rest our souls. Our salvation is grounded here. Jesus is our Saviour.

Let us however be patient. Let us reckon with this that in the process of time thought about the Person of Christ deepened. This was bound to happen. Men and women could not, cannot be stopped from reflecting on their faith, and it is not right that they should be inhibited. So after some thirty years following St Peter's simple preaching at Pentecost this is what Paul wrote to the Christians at Colossae about Christ, no doubt expecting them to understand it. 'He is the image of the invisible God, the first-born of all creation; for in him all things were created, in heaven and on earth, visible and invisible, whether thrones or dominions or principalities or authorities – all things were created through him and for him. He is before all things, and in him all things hold together' (Colossians 1.15–17 (RSV)). What a difference! Of this grand writing about Christ very little, apart from St John's Prologue, has entered into the stories about him in the gospels. This does not however make it wrong or irrelevant, on the contrary the very omission of it from the gospels contributes to our reassurance about the authenticity of the historical background which they present. They have not been substantially adjusted to suit later doctrine. Jesus is presented as people actually encountered him in Galilee and Judaea.

Now this, also important for our reassurance: one of the four gospel writers, St Luke, not only produced this kind of portrait of Jesus, protesting the trouble he had taken to make it accurate, he also wrote the book of the Acts of the Apostles showing how the Church was established and grew up on the basis of its early preaching. That it was not grand, elaborate or doctrinally involved points to the authenticity of the account. There is nothing here about the *logos* in creation, nothing about the incarnation of the *logos*, nothing about two natures in Christ, human and divine, but there is a repeated emphasis on the resurrection of Jesus. This is the starting point for an understanding of who he is.

There are people, I know, good people, who would like the simplicity of the early days of the Church to be not only the starting point of our understanding of Jesus but the finishing point. They wish St Paul had never existed. They accuse him of complicating, if not distorting, the simple faith of straightforward believers in Jesus. But the simple Gospel (so called) has implications, and very soon the early Church had to carry the Gospel of the risen Christ into a sophisticated Greek world. Questions were asked. Answers had to be given. The significance of the Gospel had to be thought through. This is what St Paul initiated.

3 THE SAVIOUR

I return now to where I began, the shepherds hearing the message of the angel, 'For unto you is born this day in the city of David a Saviour, who is Christ the Lord'. It took time for people to see the baby in the manger at Bethlehem as the saviour. It took time for them to see the Christ of Galilee and Judaea as the saviour. We all of us only ever begin to see him as such when we come round to him by way of the Cross and the Risen Christ. And only then, I think, as we look with delayed despair at the other saviours of a kind which offer themselves – and drag on disappointingly – material prosperity, social engineering, technology, politics. . . . Yes, they have their places, they require our attention and skill, but they do not reach the root of the human problem which is the flawed human heart. Unless there is a Gospel which reaches here, we have no saviour from the meaningless of life which is the condition that dogs man's best efforts today.

We, in the Church, believe that we have in the incarnate Christ this kind of saviour. This is why I make no apology for preaching as I have about Jesus. I claim to have presented no kind of rarified doctrine unsuitable for ordinary people. God became man in Christ for us, not for himself. But for us and our plight there would have been no incarnation, no baby in Bethlehem's manger, no shepherds, no wise men coming to see. '*Cur Deus Homo*' wrote Anselm, Archbishop of Canterbury in the twelfth century in the little book that bears his name – *Why did God Become Man*. And the answer is 'for us men and for our salvation'. Once grasp this and the Incarnation will no longer be a mere theological formula but the ground of our hope in what seems sometimes a hopeless world. The Incarnation is the ground of our worship of Christ and all that we do here in church, and in the lifestyle outside we endeavour to follow. We bow before him in adoration and praise because he became man for us, he took up our nature in order to be our saviour. How can we neglect him? How can we not study his life? How can we not assemble for thanksgiving?

Bless the Lord, O my soul:
and all that is within me,
bless his holy name.

16

GOD'S INITIATIVE AND OUR FAITH

'How can this be,' said Mary, 'when I have no husband?' The angel answered, 'The Holy Spirit will come upon you, and the power of the Most High will overshadow you; and for that reason the holy child to be born will be called "Son of God". . . .' 'Here am I,' said Mary; 'I am the Lord's servant; as you have spoken, so be it.' Then the angel left her.

LUKE 1.34, 35, 38 (NEB)

Unless you are an unusual person – and none the worse for that of course – you are far more interested in people and events than in theories and abstractions, which truth to tell, bore you. So let me put you at your ease, I am going to talk about an event, something which happened at a specific time and place; and, like all events, of necessity had a beginning. This is true of the incarnate life of Jesus. There had to be a human birth, a mother and a cradle, all very homely, all within our capability to understand, even children can warm to it.

1 THE VIRGIN BIRTH UNHISTORICAL

But you say to me, 'Yes, I agree, something happened but not this which these verses from St Luke describe. No human life gets a start without a male insemination. It can't. After all, for all the intensive experimentation on human embryos in recent years no medical scientist has been able to cause a virgin unaided to bear a child.' This is the end of the matter; and it certainly is if the thesis holds good that what no man or woman has ever achieved can be achieved. But what if there is a God? Is anything impossible for God?

Maybe not, but *would* God have brought someone into the world by a virginal conception completely out of alignment with his own laws of nature? And suppose a miracle child did take place – and miracle is what is involved here – would not the resulting child, and later the full-grown man, be fundamentally different, indeed alien from the rest of us, not a real man at all, not like us anyway? How then could he be our saviour if he did not share our likeness? And so on natural grounds, that is the laws of nature as we know them, and also on religious grounds, the story of the Virgin Birth as set out by St Luke has to be rejected as unhistorical.

2 THE VIRGIN BIRTH AS POETIC INTERPRETATION

So what action do we take? Deposit it in the dustbin? Should we not however be wise and treat it as a beautiful legend, as poetry, maybe the product of pious imagination, devised with the express purpose of setting Jesus up on a pinnacle proclaiming that he was no ordinary man, not even simply an exceedingly good man and a remarkable man for he was more? The Greeks did much the same when they invented supernatural births for their heroes. Christmas on this view can remain, we can still put up the holly and the ivy, and give our family and friends presents. As intelligent twentieth-century people in a scientific technological age we can on this view interpret St Luke's Christmas story of the Virgin Birth of Jesus as we do any other great work of literary art, and St Luke's narrative is certainly that, we shall not take it literally.

Now someone is uneasy. This story is different. It is in the Bible, it is part of Scripture. Yes, but not even the New Testament makes much of it. Only two of the four gospels report it, St Matthew and St Luke. St Mark and St John appear to know nothing of it at all. And St Paul, than whom was none more determined to set out the essentials of the Christian Gospel, makes no reference to it whatsoever. So need we be uneasy in letting the Virgin Birth of Jesus drop out of our Christian confession?

3 THE VIRGIN BIRTH AS A SAFEGUARD

Nevertheless, to be honest, I have to admit that I am still uneasy, even though I recognize the argument of those who declare that it is possible to believe in the incarnation of Christ without accepting the Virgin Birth as historical. I recognize that we can truthfully declare: Yes, we believe in the Incarnation, but we do not presume to know *how* it came about, we neither affirm it nor deny it, we leave it so to speak, in the pending file. Nevertheless, I repeat, I have to admit to being uneasy with this reasonable agnosticism. On these grounds: the Virgin Birth safeguards the divine initiative in our salvation and without that divine initiative we have no salvation. Let me spell this out. Suppose Joseph and Mary married and decided to have a family. Or suppose after some months of marriage Mary was found to be pregnant, would not the child have been born because of the will of the parents, or the impulse of the parents? So what becomes of the divine initiative? In that situation Jesus would be the child of *human* initiative. But this runs clearly contrary to the New Testament teaching that our salvation issues from the initiative of God. St Paul put it as clear as clear could be in his letter to the Galatians, one of the first books in the New Testament to be written, if not the first, 'But when the time had fully come, *God sent forth his Son*, born of woman' (4.4).

I am tempted to go on with the argument but to do so would be unwise. After all this is not a theological lecture but a sermon and I fancy I can hear the reaction of not a few to what I have said already, 'Oh, I can't be bothered with all these arguments and counter arguments, I prefer to accept the story of Jesus' birth as it stands. It has a reassuring message for me about God and this is all I ask.'

4 THE NATURE OF FAITH

So let us return to the text of St Luke, chapter 1, verses 34 and following, and in particular Mary's words when the apparently fantastic news of the birth of the Saviour child to her was announced. She questioned it as well she might, all of which goes to show that our questions about it, tiresome as they may be, are not unreasonable. Mary herself questioned it. But she replied, 'I am the Lord's servant; as you have spoken, so be it'. This is acceptance, acceptance in the absolute. It is the human response which allows God to act, a response wholly compounded of faith, faith in a word of promise, nothing else, absolutely nothing else. Not one single word about Mary to qualify her for bearing the Christ child. She is neither described as pious nor pure nor worthy, which is not to say she wasn't all of these, but to this day, she is largely an unknown character. She became the mother of Jesus because she accepted the promise made to her by God's angel, 'The Holy Spirit will come upon you, and the power of the Most High will overshadow you; and for that reason the holy child to be born will be called "Son of God" '. Who would believe such a word? but Mary did believe it, 'I am the Lord's servant', she said, 'as you have spoken, so be it'. Acceptance of the word is the reason why Mary became the mother of the Son of God, that and absolutely nothing else.

And now another point. This bareness of the Annunciation Scripture is eloquent about what faith is. Faith in its essence is response, response to God's word of promise. Faith is not primarily feeling, not even religious feeling, this could indicate superstition. Nor does the study of religion of itself indicate faith, it could be intellectualism. Nor is faith the same as activitism in charitable works. Faith is quite different. It is acceptance. It is the response 'Yes' to God's word of promise, a gracious promise wholly unmerited.

Because this is so faith implies hearing. As St Paul wrote in his letter to the Romans (10.17), 'Faith comes by hearing and hearing by the word of God'. What we need to hear is the word of God's promises. For example, 'Fear not: for I have redeemed thee, I have called thee by thy name; thou art mine. When thou passest through the waters, I will be with thee; and through the rivers, they shall not overflow thee: when thou walkest through the fire, thou shalt not be burned; neither shall the flame kindle upon thee. For I am the Lord thy God, the Holy One of Israel, thy Saviour' (Isaiah 43.1–3). Or again, 'Be not afraid; for behold, I bring you good tidings of great joy, which shall be to all people: for there is born this day in the city of David a Saviour, which is Christ the Lord' (Luke 2.10, 11). Faith is hearing these divine words of promise and saying 'Yes' to them. This is acceptance and this is faith. Mary provides the most shining example of all time. She said to the angel, 'As you have spoken, so be it'.

5 THE OUTCOME OF FAITH

And what was the outcome? Need we ask? Christ was born of Mary. We love the story. He was cradled in a manger at Bethlehem with, maybe, the oxen and the asses standing by. And this is the message for us. When we say 'Yes' to God's words of his promises to us, that is when we accept them, then the Spirit of Christ is born in our hearts, and even becomes manifest in our lives among the shopping baskets, brooms and Hoovers, office desks and computers and motor cars standing by the door. The Spirit of Christ is born among us when, like Mary, we accept God's word of promise. The miracle of transformed people happens through faith, not through intellectualism, nor through moralism, nor through striving, nor social activism, but through faith.

6 A CONFESSION

I want to hold on to the doctrine of the Virgin Birth as in the Nicene Creed, 'I believe in one Lord Jesus Christ: 'Who for us men and our salvation came down from heaven, And was incarnate by the Holy Ghost of the Virgin Mary, And was made man. . . .' The Christian Church has kept its grip on this for well-nigh two thousand years though sometimes with shaky hands. I want to hold on to it as a safeguard of *God's initiative* in our salvation. I count this to be essential. I also want to hold on to it in order to preserve the stature of Mary the mother of Jesus. If Jesus had been born in the ordinary way of Joseph and Mary would Mary have needed the exercise of faith with only the word of God on which to rely? And for that matter, would Joseph have suffered the agonies he did? I want to reverence Mary. I want a very high place for Joseph and Mary in the working out of God's purposes for us all. And so for all the poetry, legend and editing there may well be in the birth narratives of Jesus provided by St Matthew and St Luke I think wisdom begs us recognize beneath it all an historical event. This strange beginning, I am driven to think, happened.

17
ST MATTHEW'S STORY

Now the birth of Jesus Christ took place in this way.
MATTHEW 1.18 (RSV)

I am going to ask you to look at the birth narratives of Jesus as they have been handed down to us. Yes, I know about the problems, but still I ask you to look at them *as they are* and how we hear them read in church. Too often we become so occupied with the problems that we fail to do this. After all if nothing else they are literary masterpieces.

1 A SCENE OF UNCERTAINTY

First St Matthew's story. It presents a scene of uncertainty, misunderstanding, if not darkness that can almost be felt. This was the setting in which the Incarnation took place. It centres upon Joseph, an honest, kindly, village carpenter. Was there ever a love more uncomplicated than that which filled his whole being for Mary the village girl? They were deeply in love, they had their plans for marriage. Their days were radiant in anticipation. And then all their serenity was shattered. Mary was pregnant. Joseph could not believe it. It made no sense. How could a girl like Mary get trapped in this condition? If you have imagination you can see the poor man at night after the day's work was done pacing up and down his bleak room. What should he do? What could he do? He could not marry her bearing someone else's child, and whose? In God's name, whose! But to be rid of her would tear out his tender heart. He could not live without Mary. And the horrible publicity of it that must inevitably be all but broke this sensitive man. And where was Mary now? He couldn't find Mary. A horror of thick darkness settled on Joseph. And then it happened. An angel appeared to Joseph in a dream. Yes, an angel. And wherever angels are made to enter the biblical stories they are there to warn us. Pay attention! Be careful. You have come to a frontier of mystery. You can penetrate no further. Either you believe or you turn back. What the angel said was, 'Fear not to take unto thee Mary to be thy wife, for that which is conceived in her is of the Holy Spirit'. Did Joseph believe it? Would you believe it? St Matthew tells us Joseph did believe. He caught up with Mary. He married Mary and she bore a child whom, according to the angel's instructions, they called Jesus.

But was this the end of the agony? Do you think for one moment that the tittle-tattle ceased when they were married? Don't forget all this took place in a small community set with traditions and taboos. Is it likely that anyone accepted the explanation of the Virgin Birth, that Mary's child was God's child conceived by the agency of the Holy Spirit? Could there possibly be an absence of snide remarks, whispers behind cupped hands and knowing winks? All this for Joseph and Mary, sensitive souls, was horrible. I tell you, the picture St Matthew offers us of the nativity of Jesus is almost wholly dark. Jesus was cradled in an environment of mocking unbelief.

So must we put away the tinsel and the jollity in celebrating Christmas? Certainly not. There was joy, of course there was joy. How Mary's face must have lit up as she cuddled her little baby! and how Joseph's heart was gladdened to see his wife's serenity! And how reassuring that a tiny few sensed the uniqueness of this child, acting as they offered their adoration like kings bringing gifts of gold, frankincense and myrrh. But all around was a climate of malediction which in time, so it was rumoured, crystallized into the suspicion of Herod, the King, himself, ever with an ear cocked for rumours of rivals. So Joseph fled to Egypt, and St Matthew presents us with the astonishing picture of Joseph saving the Saviour, a refugee on the road journeying south.

2 BARE SURVIVAL

What does this story of bare survival of the infant Jesus say? Surely that the Incarnation came about as an event not only in obscurity but in an atmosphere of suspicion and in circumstances of physical danger. Only a tiny few welcomed it. St Matthew's blunt words put the situation in a nutshell, 'Herod sought the life of the young child to destroy him'.

I need to make the point here that for a considerable number of early Christians, Christians from a Jewish background, which we might call the Palestinian Church, this sombre account of the birth of Jesus was the only one available to them. They did not have our four gospels. The New Testament did not come into existence till much later. They had no access to St Luke's story of the baby in the manger. St Matthew wrote of the story of Jesus' birth as he knew it and it presented a picture of a costly incarnation in terms of misunderstanding, suspicion and danger. There was no platform, no trumpets and very little rejoicing. Jesus began in the precariousness and fragility of existence at the lower, if not lowest level of society, a refugee, but he survived. Of course he survived. Whatever the dangers no one is at risk who is in the line of God's purposes, they cannot be.

3 A FIRST-CENTURY JEW

And now this boring genealogy with which St Matthew has prefixed his nativity account. At least, most readers of the New Testament are bored with it. A string of names! What a way to begin a story! What would be the reaction to a sermon begun in this fashion? But my guess is that those for whom St Matthew wrote in the first place pounced on it with alacrity. Was Jesus a true Jew? Had he an honourable pedigree? Was Joseph really a descendant of the royal Davidic line? And so St Matthew constructed this genealogy to satisfy his readers. Joseph's pedigree was impeccable notwithstanding some of the lapses of his forebears. They are not glossed over. So from the start, no, before the start, Jesus was not separate from sinners. His readers were satisfied.

But are we satisfied? Would we not expect the saviour of the world to be a Universal Man, neither Jew nor Greek, neither black nor white, neither oriental nor occidental, in other words racially neutral, some might want to add neither male nor female, but both? Then anyone, anywhere, at any time could relate to him, the Supreme Unconditioned Man! But in that case would the Incarnation have taken place? Would Jesus have been a real man and not an artificial one? Jesus, says the genealogy, was racially conditioned; he had a Jewish face, a Jewish accent and was nurtured in the Jewish tradition. All of which means that God makes himself known in the particular, and not in the general; in the concrete and not in the abstract, in the personal and not in the theoretical. It is a point we might do well to remind those educationalists who would have children presented at the outset of their learning process with a whole variety of religions. It will not work. We must begin with the particular, and then maybe expand to the general. And all of us will only encounter the real God in the concrete circumstances of our lives and in racially, culturally, sexually *conditioned* people. Philosophy has its place, abstract reasoning a proper function but the God who confronts us with grace and demand comes with the face and tongue of a first-century Galilean man. This is what Incarnation involves. This is the challenge and awkwardness of the Christian Gospel.

Someone wishes to stand up and complain. You say, Mr Preacher, that God assumed human flesh, God became a man, the Incarnation was designed so that we might know God, but of what use can this be to the majority of the human race who cannot, in the nature of the case see this man, hear his voice or touch his hands? We have no idea what he looked like or what was the timbre of his voice. What value if what is supposed to be revealed remains behind a screen? But we have the testimony of those who did see him and touch him as the first verse of the first epistle of St John in the New Testament eloquently declares. And the indisputable fact stands that Jesus of Nazareth is well-known today throughout the world in all manner of contrasting situations. And this must be added. It may be to our advantage, I think it is, that with all our diverse value and cultural ideas we do *not* know what he looked like nor what was the timbre of his voice, indeed the very lack enables us to see him in a form pleasing to our *particular* eyes and ears. *In this way* this particular man does become the Universal Man, the Ideal yet real man. All men and women everywhere from the frozen north to the torrid equatorial lands can and do equate with him. This is the miracle of the Incarnate Christ.

I come back to the anguish which is the setting for St Matthew's account of the birth of Jesus. We must not rub this out. Incarnation involves it. And note this, if you take away the problematical Virgin Birth, and it is problematical, if you make Joseph the natural father of Jesus you must reckon with this, that you take away the stature of Joseph who against the odds held on to the miracle of Jesus' birth. I would like to leave you, as a result of this sermon, thinking of Joseph. A sermon is not meant to be a theological lecture but a call for a response. If you believe the Incarnation, and as a Christian you must, expect misunderstanding, incredulity and perhaps ridicule on the part of some who reject it. And in the face of contemporary secularism you yourself will have a struggle to hold to it. St Matthew reminds us that the Incarnation faced all this *from the beginning*, and so it has been ever since. But he showed us Joseph, that humble, faithful man. What better could we do than emulate Joseph? Joseph believed.

18

ST LUKE'S STORIES

And she [Mary] brought forth her firstborn son, and wrapped him in swaddling clothes, and laid him in a manger; because there was no room for them in the inn.

LUKE 2.7 (AV)

1 DOWN TO SENTIMENTALITY

This is St Luke's account of the nativity. We love it. Christmas would be empty without the little baby cradled in the straw of the manger; and if we must add the ox, the ass and the camel standing by, so be it though they are not mentioned in the account. Please do not misunderstand me. I am far from being a sceptic about these stories but I have to acknowledge that even if the whole narrative is an invention it is a winner, a superb piece of fiction. It catches hold of the human heart. Anyone who has watched children, especially of course little girls, peeping into our Christmas cribs to catch a glimpse of 'baby Jesus' will know the pull. The scene is almost irresistible. Anyone with even a spark of humanity left in 'him' – I said 'him' – must at least be touched by this. You can of course call it an appeal to sentiment, and so it is, perhaps mere sentiment. If so this is the point I want to drive home. God in the Incarnation comes right down, down, down to the level of sentiment so as to touch the very humblest of us, even people with very little in the way of reasoning powers, even little children.

My attention has been caught these last few years now that I have time to help with the weekly shopping at the local supermarket to watch the women in the queues as I stand waiting my turn at the check-out point. Should a mother arrive with a baby in her arms all activity on the part of the women ceases. They all move over to peep at the baby. I have seen the girl checking our purchases quit her stool and pricing mechanism for one quick look and one swift cooing. I am not laughing. I am deadly serious. I ask myself, could God possibly have become more accessible, more evocative to a response than appearing on the world's scene as a helpless infant? Incarnation really does mean God stooping down to where we are.

I met a man a few years back who had attended an exhibition in Russia for the glorification of Lenin. What really caught his attention among all the show pieces was a baby in a cradle, baby Lenin, the birthplace of the new era of Communism. Stolen from the Christian tradition? Stolen to fill the gap left by the cancellation of the Bethlehem scenes? Possibly, but more likely this exhibit was seen as a way of coming close to the human heart along the path of sentiment and so winning allegiance.

You will see from this that I want to retain the sentimentality of Christmas. It is because I want to retain the reality of the Incarnation, the totality of God's coming down to our level. I am not surprised that more people attend churches at Christmas than at Easter; though Easter is the greater Christian festival, Christmas is easier to grasp. So let us be thankful to St Luke, who must have trailed all over Galilee and Judaea to pick up the material for his nativity stories and somehow come close to Mary the mother of Jesus; she would not readily divulge her story, but he was a doctor. I know I am not on sure ground when I make these suggestions but they are not unreasonable. I simply repeat, let us be grateful to St Luke for his heart-touching nativity stories. How much poorer we would be with only St Mark's gospel which contains no birth narrative at all, and St John's gospel with its place taken by a profound theological prologue. Yes, each gospel has a distinctive significance, and maybe in a way St Luke's is the least profound of all four, but it is more human. There the Incarnation stands out and not only in the birth narrative.

2 A DATED ACCOUNT

We turn now from this and consider two other chief characteristics of St Luke's gospel. First it is a dated account. The Incarnation began in the days of Caesar Augustus at the time he called for a census, the first under the Syrian governorship of Quirinius. Now those of us who have had to study these matters in detail know about the uncertainty surrounding the precise dating of these enrolments, and we know about the almost endless learned discussions of the theological and literary critics as to whether St Luke wrote as an historian or as a theologian. I do not want to weary you with these, nor indeed do I want to weary myself, though I am not so foolish as to 'rubbish' them. This, however, I do not think anyone can gainsay: St Luke intended us to understand that the story of

Jesus' birth is historical even if the *precise* dating may not be. Like any good writer (and St Luke was that) he structured his account and that artistically, but the nativity of Jesus is not a fairy story, nor wholly legendary, there is no 'once-upon-a-timeness' about it. The Incarnation happened. Christianity is an historical religion, not a myth, and judging from the fact that at verse 5, chapter 1, in his gospel St Luke breaks off a near classical style of Greek into one with distinct Semitisms, it looks as if he was drawing his material from local traditions. It was not the entire product of his own subtle and artistic imagination.

3 THE HUMBLE CIRCUMSTANCES

And now another characteristic. St Luke was at pains in his account to stress the humble circumstances of the nativity of Jesus. Mary's baby was cradled in a manger where the animals, mainly asses, were stabled and fed, a makeshift business, and all because there was no room in the *kataluma* (whatever that may be) at Bethlehem's inn. My guess is it was the lower ground room jostling with travellers displaced on account of the Imperial census requirements, and there simply was no space for the couple, Joseph and Mary, to bed down. And would the jostling crowd appreciate a woman about to deliver a child? and would she herself want it? I suggest both Joseph and Mary accepted that relatively private corner of the stable with its manger with gratitude, thankful for small mercies. I find no grounds in the story for suggesting that the innkeeper was a churlish fellow who turned them out. He was probably at his wits' end with the sudden influx of jabbering, protesting travellers. Did Joseph act as midwife at the birth of Jesus? You can't go much lower than that at a birth. Then Mary wrapped her baby round in what we traditionally call 'swaddling clothes' which she must have brought with her from Nazareth to Bethlehem, some eighty miles, in case. . . .

But need she have come to Bethlehem? Could she not have remained in Nazareth profiting at the birth by the assistance of kindly neighbours? The census did not require the wife to attend her husband at the enrolment in the place from which he originated. Joseph could have gone alone. But were there kindly neighbours? Could it be that Mary ran the obvious risk to her pregnancy by travelling with Joseph rather than endure alone the ostracism and perhaps insults of the local community because of the secrecy concerning her child's origin? Villagers are hostile to secrecy on their doorstep. Such was the nadir of Joseph and Mary's experience to which the Incarnation had brought them. For them it was humiliating.

4 ORDINARINESS

The other point to which I would draw your attention is the sheer ordinariness of the preliminaries to Jesus' birth. St Luke begins with a story of Zacharias and Elizabeth, a right-living but dull couple if ever there was one, orthodox and staid, nothing out of line, nothing the slightest bit wayward, good-living Jews who kept the law blamelessly, fulfilling their appointed duties even though they had eaten their hearts out because they had no child. It was to this house and home that Mary fled when the annunciation was made to her of her child to be. These were her kinsfolk. Theirs was the kind of lifestyle in which Mary was at home. It is one little window on her character. So Jesus was born in the lowliest of circumstances and nurtured in a home and atmosphere of orthodox religion. Be careful then how you count Jesus a radical, he was an initiator, he was a free man, but he neither began nor lived his whole life sitting loose to the religious orthodoxy of his cultural environment. Joseph and Mary led him from the outset in this way and he kept to it. After eight days he was presented as a baby in the Temple according to the Law, the only offering this humble couple could afford being a mere brace of pigeons. Did even the vergers (if they had vergers in the Temple) bother to notice them? But two pairs of eyes penetrated the obscurity, old eyes, a man Simeon and a woman Anna, they saw in the little bundle in Mary's arms the saviour of the world. Did they sense the Incarnation? No, I cannot tell you other than what St Luke says. You can do as you like with the information. I recommend that at least you treat it with respect.

5 MY CONFESSION

Perhaps you will complain that in this sermon I have been divulging how I personally read these nativity stories. You may charge me with a naive reading of them. You may charge me with too critical a reading of them. So be it. I believe in the Incarnation and I have said how. I am committed to it in faith. There is much I do not pretend to understand. At the end of the day belief is what matters, not understanding nor even assent because it is in the doctrine of the Church, though this is not to be despised. We only live as Christians by *personal trust* in the living Christ who became 'incarnate for us men and for our salvation'. What I try to do as a preacher is help my hearers to believe; and this I have come to know, that faith kindles faith. This is why I have set out, albeit sketchily, how I personally believe these admittedly difficult nativity stories which St Matthew and St Luke have given us. It is so that we may trust.

19
THE INCARNATE LOGOS

In the beginning was the Word, and the Word was with God, and the Word was God. He was in the beginning with God; all things were made through him, and without him was not anything made that was made. In him was life, and the life was the light of men. The light shines in the darkness, and the darkness has not overcome it.

JOHN 1.1–5 (RSV)

Anyone who is called upon to make a speech, perhaps at a wedding reception, or at some public meeting, anyone who has to preach a sermon – and not only clergy perform this ministry nowadays – anyone who feels the urge to write a book, will be well advised to pay the closest possible attention to how they start; the beginning is all important. In broadcasting a speaker must give the impression in the first thirty seconds that he is authoritative and is going to be interesting, otherwise the viewers and listeners will switch off.

1 THE MEANING OF LOGOS

Now at the risk of sounding irreverent the writer of the fourth gospel, St John's gospel, had to watch this point. He was burning to write an interpretive account of Jesus of Nazareth but for whom? In the first instance for his readers in Ephesus. But this was a place mainly of Greek culture, not Jewish. How hopeless then to begin his gospel by writing about Jesus as the promised Messiah. Greeks were not looking for a Messiah, least of all a Jewish one. And they would be equally bored with the story of a virgin birth; they had stories in plenty of the supernatural births of their heroes at which they smiled tolerantly; and as for a Jewish genealogy, which is the introduction St Matthew provided for his gospel designed for readers with a Jewish background, this was out of the question. So he put pen to paper and opened his gospel with a reference to a broad basic principle of the Universe as every intelligent Greek understood it, namely Rationality. All the laws of nature by which it works, sunrise and sunset, the phases of the moon, seed time and harvest, all are particular manifestations of the one great underlying principle of Rationality, the very opposite of chaos, they called it *Logos*. So this is what St John wrote as the opening of his book, 'At the root of everything is Logos'.

Now these words could equally well be read as 'In the beginning was the Word', and this is how readers with a Jewish, and not Greek, background understood them. Their minds flashed back at once to the opening sentence of the Bible, 'In the beginning God created the heavens and the earth'. So in this intriguing way St John gripped the attention from the very start of both intellectual Greeks and religious Jews. Clearly this book would not be some simple story about Jesus. There would indeed be a story but with profound hidden depths. It would tell of God, but not as inscrutable, passive and dumb. God is at the root of all the operations in the natural order, and this would have to include the evolutionary process. He expresses himself in word and action. He is Light and he is Life. The world we know and where he manifests himself is mysterious and often dark and repelling, nature is 'red in tooth and claw' but his presence is never wholly obliterated, there is no single man, woman or child in whom there is not an inkling of his light.

Tremendous themes these! And here and there in the gospel they are developed under the guise of apparently simple stories about Jesus. And as if this were not enough to stir the reader's attention this Logos, this divine principle of Being or Existence, familiar to philosophical thinkers, actually took on a human personality and lived among us. He was truth itself but not in the least forbidding. The writer, along with others, saw this himself. It came to be called the Incarnation. Surely this prologue to the Fourth Gospel was enough to cause those who read it, and appreciated what it was saying, either to collapse in guffaws of ridicule, Jesus as the Logos! What on earth next? or to have their eyes opened to a completely new way of understanding time and eternity.

2 THREE CHARACTERISTICS OF THE LOGOS

Let us now touch on these deep themes of St John's gospel hinted at in the Prologue, bearing in mind that the Prologue here is not simply an introduction to the book but a summary of its message.

First the creative energy of the Logos or Word of God. 'All

things were made through him, and without him was not anything made that was made.' This creative power became incarnate, hence the pronoun 'him' and not 'it' as expected. 'And the Logos or Word became flesh and dwelt, [tabernacled] among us', a temporary lodging as in a tent. 'And we beheld his glory, glory as of the only begotten of the Father, full of grace and truth.' And you turn over a page of the gospel, and there he is, the incarnate Christ, at a wedding feast. The wine has run out, but with a word six great stone jars of water are turned into wine, splendid wine, wine in abundance, just like the abundance of nature. It is an event so unlikely we need only a tiny temptation to explain it away. John, however, the author of the gospel calls it a sign, the first of seven which he provides in his narrative. Of what is it a sign? What does the event point to in the person of Jesus? It indicates the creative power of the Logos.

Second, 'In him', that is in the Logos, 'was life'. So states the Prologue. And you turn over a couple of pages in the gospel and there is Jesus back again in Cana of Galilee, but this time not at a bubbling wedding party but confronted by an official with anguish stamped all over his face because his son is at the point of death. 'Sir, come down before my child dies', is the urgent plea. And all Jesus did was to speak words, 'Go your way, your son will live'. And the boy did live. When the official arrived back home down in Capernaum by the lake he found life in his home not death. On this event John commented, 'This is the second sign that Jesus did when he had come from Judaea to Galilee'. Again we ask, Sign? Sign of what? The life principle of the divine Logos or Word of God incarnate in Jesus.

Third, 'In him was life, and the life was the light of men'. Life and Light. They go together. I am a bit of a gardener. I wouldn't rate myself any higher than that, but this I know, plants will not grow unless they have light. You will have noticed that the first words in the Creation narrative of Genesis 1 are 'Let there be light'. Only after this creative act is there life upon the earth. Turning to the gospels we read of Jesus opening the eyes of the blind so that they can see light and begin to lead a full life to replace their former stumbling in the dark. In St John's gospel faith is equivalent to seeing the light. So the blind man whose healing story is recounted at some length in chapter 9 comes to see Jesus as the Son of man and to believe in him. Jesus then is the light of the Logos, the light incarnate, indeed 'the light of the world'. (John 8.12).

Does all this sound fanciful? But no rosy view of the world is provided by the writer of this Prologue, there is realism here. 'The light shines in the darkness.' Not after this verse can the Incarnation be loosely conceived of as the immanence of God in nature so that nature can be romanticized as divine, much less that God equals nature and nature equals God. No, the light shines in the darkness. It does not even shine in a sphere of neutrality. Evil stalks abroad. But the light still shines. It has always shone even before the coming of Christ, but with him the shining is brilliant, at times dazzling. It does not however dispel the darkness, that time is not yet, it pierces through the darkness like a searchlight. The darkness even swirled around Jesus, its thickest at the cross of Calvary. 'And when the sixth hour had come, there was darkness over the whole land until the ninth hour' (Mark 15.33). But the darkness did not obliterate the light, it never has. As the Prologue puts it, 'the light shines in the darkness, and the darkness has not overtaken it'. Nor has the darkness of the world dispersed. Deception, cruelty and greed stalk the earth. The battle of light with darkness goes on.

3 TWO FURTHER IMPLICATIONS

Now two further points from the Prologue about the Logos. 'The true light that enlightens every man was coming into the world.' So runs verse 9. It is so sweeping it almost takes our breath away. As the creative power of the Logos is responsible for the existence of all things so its illumination is responsible for the light that enlightens all human beings. There is no one, there never has been anyone in whom the light as mind and conscience has not at least flickered, sometimes more than flickered, gloriously more. No coarse savage, no criminal, no idolater, no sensualist; and on a different level altogether, no adherent of a religion or sect other than the one to which we have given ourselves, but the light of the Logos is there. This is why we must have regard for all human beings of whatever class, creed, colour or conviction. This is why we must give room for the faiths other than the Christian; something of the light of the Logos shines in them all. It is the light which came to expression in the incarnate Christ, the light of the Logos.

Four sombre verses about the universal enlightening follow. 'He was in the world, and the world was made through him, yet the world knew him not. He came to his own home, and his own people received him not.' Then the rejection lifts. 'But to all who received him, who believed in his name, he gave power to become children of God; who were born, not of blood nor of the will of the flesh nor of the will of man, but of God.' Note this last sentence. It declares that all who become children of God by believing 'in his name' become so not through their own human effort, will or impulse but by God's initiative. One early manuscript of the gospel at this point reads not 'who *were* born' but 'who was born' making it a reference to the Virgin Birth. Almost certainly this is not what John wrote, but it is hard to think that this particular wording was not influenced by belief in the Virgin Birth. As he was born 'not of blood nor of the will of the flesh nor of the will of man, but of God', so God's children become his children by belief in Christ's name. Turn over two or three pages more in the gospel and we find Jesus saying as much to Nicodemus. We have to be born 'from above'.

Come back to where we began. 'At the root of everything is Logos.' And the Greek-thinking people nodded approval. 'In the beginning was the Word.' And the people with a Hebrew background nodded approval. But the writer did not stop there. He went on 'And the Logos became flesh and dwelt among us'. Could the Greeks believe that? Could the Hebrews? Some did. They did so on the testimony of a small group of people who were eyewitnesses of Jesus. They testified to him as the Incarnate Christ. They preached him. And out of their preaching, and the coming of the Holy Spirit, the Church grew.

20

THE INCARNATE CHRIST STILL ENCOUNTERS US

I came from the Father and have come into the world. Now I am leaving the world again and going to the Father.

JOHN 16.28 (NEB)

I have to begin this sermon on a solemn note. I am sorry about this but I have no alternative because it has to concern itself with the ending of the incarnate life of Christ. Most of us hate goodbyes in any form – children going away to school, friends taking up residence in another place on account of a change of work, and more poignant still, much more poignant, the death of someone to whom we are closely bound. It is the finality that hurts, the realization that they will not be seen again, only a memory will remain.

Now Jesus went away. In his conversation with his disciples in the Upper Room the night before his crucifixion, according to St John's account, he gave them clearly to understand that this was about to happen. 'I came from the Father and have come into the world. Now I am leaving the world again and going to the Father.' Of course they were sad, desperately sad. And I do not suppose they found much relief in this further comment, 'Nevertheless I tell you the truth: it is for your good that I am leaving you. If I do not go, your Advocate will not come, whereas if I go, I will send him to you.' Did they understand that he was speaking to them of the coming of the Holy Spirit? And if they did, which I doubt, would this help them in their bereavement? I doubt this too. When we lose a familiar bodily presence it is not much comfort to be told we shall have a spiritual presence.

And here is the problem for us now in a nutshell. If the Incarnation took place in the man Jesus with the express purpose that we might know God through hearing, seeing and touching him, this was all very well for his contemporaries, but how will it avail us now? And if because we are creatures of flesh and blood, that is to say *embodied* spirits, only able adequately to receive the revelation when it appears in a bodily form, where does this leave the mass of mankind when that bodily form, conceived to be necessary, is no longer with us? To express the situation bluntly, the incarnation of Christ came to an end so where are we now?

We have, I suggest, three ways in which we can encounter Christ – in the coming of the Holy Spirit, in the study of the scriptures, and in sacramental worship of the Church. Let us look at these three ways in turn recognizing how they overlap each other.

1 THE HOLY SPIRIT

First, the coming of the Holy Spirit. Now the Holy Spirit is the Spirit of Christ. He is in the world. He has always been in the world but not as the Spirit of the incarnate Christ. This could not be till the life and work of the incarnate Christ was completed, that is, including the crucifixion and resurrection. Then it was – to use symbolic language – that he received the crown of glory and ascended with great triumph to his throne in heaven.

How, without sounding puerile, can I throw light on this so that it can, even in a measure, be grasped? I will run the risk, preachers have to run risks sometimes. Here then is a bright boy from an average home in the suburbs. He wins a scholarship from his primary school to a grammar school, and then to Oxford. Yes, his old schools are proud of him, they talk about him, and some boys try to emulate his success; but his name is not on everyone's lips till he has become a member of the Cabinet and a statesman with a European reputation. Then his influence is worldwide.

A weak illustration? Yes, I know, but what can I do? Jesus began in obscurity but there came a time when his name, *Jesus as Lord*, had spread across the Roman Empire. Why? Because the Cross and Resurrection had crowned his work and provided a gospel for everyone. The Resurrection was God's acceptance of what he had done, and by it the Spirit of God, the Holy Spirit was loosed into the world in a dynamic way as never before.

People caught the Spirit, ordinary people; race, sex and status were no barriers. It was the Spirit of Christ they caught, quite unlike the spirit in the world. It was caught, and still is caught through contact with individuals in whom is the Spirit, but more commonly and widespreadly through the fellowship of the Christian Church. All who are open to the Spirit become open to Christ, open to the incarnate Christ, he is a real person to them although unheard, unseen and untouched in any bodily or physical way. Time and place play no part in this as they did during the incarnate life of Christ on earth. No wonder Jesus said to his disciples, 'It is good for you that I am leaving you'. The incarnate Christ through the Spirit becomes the universal Christ available to us all.

2 THE SCRIPTURES

Now the scriptures. We have in mind of course mainly, though not exclusively, the New Testament, for the New Testament cannot be fully understood except against the background of the Old Testament. Christianity came into the world as a regenerating Spirit which people caught but it could have no lasting future were it not firmly rooted in the historical events from which it arose, namely the life, death and resurrection of Jesus. Christianity cannot bypass, cut loose, or neglect constant attention to its history. This history therefore had to be told. It had to be told by those who had lived close to it and were therefore witnesses. And it had to be written down, and it was, not much more than thirty years after the crucifixion and resurrection. The first account came from the pen of St Mark, and not long after from St Matthew and St Luke and towards the end of the first century from St John. These accounts are not biographies in the normal sense; that they are called 'gospels' marks out their peculiarity as writings. They are proclamations, they preach Christ by recounting what he did and said. If then we are to know the incarnate Christ now, it is to these gospels we must turn, we have no alternative.

And this is the extraordinary fact about them. When they are read by those who call themselves Christians, whether as individuals or in the Christian community, where the Spirit dwells, they take on a vibrant life. The incarnate Christ becomes a real presence to the hearer or the reader. What is more, when these scriptures are opened up in preaching they take on the character or function of the Word of God. What we encounter is not bare history, much less dead history, but a dynamic Person. Christianity lives because of the Holy Spirit, and it also lives because of the scriptures.

3 THE SACRAMENTAL WORSHIP OF THE CHURCH

Now the sacramental worship of the Church, and here I have chiefly in mind the Holy Communion. When in the Upper Room Jesus made plain to his disciples that he was about to leave them, or in the words of my text, 'I came from the Father and have come into the world. Now I am leaving the world again, and going to the Father', he left them with more than words, he bequeathed something they could see, touch and taste. He took bread, broke it and gave it to them. He poured out wine and passed it into their hands to drink. He said, 'This is my body, this is my blood. Do this in remembrance of me.' As in the Incarnation he took a physical body to reveal his divine presence, so he took the material substances of bread and wine as the means, or vehicles, of his future presence. This is the sacramental principle, the spiritual mediated through the material. Is it any wonder therefore that the Holy Communion is called Holy, and the elements used for it counted to be sacred? The incarnate Christ was the sacrament in Judaea and Galilee, and the consecrated bread and wine are the sacrament of his presence now.

Sacraments are visible. They can be seen. For most people what is seen makes a greater impression than what is heard. Hence the greater power of television as compared with sound radio. So in the Christian ministry the medium is not only words but a table set out and vessels for the offerings of bread and wine. They can be seen and handled. Not everyone is able to read the scriptures, not everyone is able to 'take in' what is said in a sermon be it never so straightforward, it passes them by. But something seen, decorated perhaps and made colourful, that is different, it impinges. And something to do with the feet, hands and mouth brings the spiritual within the range of a greater range of people than is the case with what is only spoken and heard. I said 'only' because words are spoken with the sacrament. Jesus spoke when he instituted the Holy Communion. It was not, it never is, a dumb show. What is more the scriptures are quoted or read as part of the occasion.

All this is clear but there are differences of interpretation, and these have to be faced. How shall the bread and the wine in the Holy Communion be understood? Are they still bread and wine after consecration to this special purpose of being the sacramental body and blood of Christ? They certainly continue to look like ordinary bread and wine and taste like ordinary bread and wine, not in the least like flesh and blood.

Now there are some Christians who believe that in spite of this obvious fact nevertheless there is a change of substance though not of appearance. I have to confess to an inability myself to subscribe to this explanation. At the other extreme are some Christians who maintain that there is no divine presence in any sense in the elements of bread and wine after their consecration, they remain bread and wine. In their view it is the faith of the communicant that makes the elements become the vehicles of God's presence to them. Again I have to confess that I do not go along with this understanding of the sacrament. I associate myself in these matters with those who believe that because the sacraments are a means of grace, God's grace, it is God himself who takes up the elements of bread and wine through which to approach us in the Holy Communion. Of course our response of faith is necessary, otherwise the sacraments are reduced to the level of magic, but it is not our faith, not our response, but God's grace, God's power, which has the initiative.

Are the sacraments then all extensions of the Incarnation? It was God's purpose to make himself known to us through the man Jesus, a physical presence. When therefore he left the world to return to the Father, are the sacraments which have a physical, material form the appointed substitute? Are they extensions of the Incarnation? Are they God's way, God who is Spirit, of making himself known to us who are physical bodies? Perhaps the argument could be sustained, and certainly is sustained in some churches, but from Christ's words in the Upper Room the night before his crucifixion the coming of the Holy Spirit seems to be the way in which the incarnation of Christ has its ministry extended beyond his life on earth. It is the Holy Spirit who is operative in the Holy Communion in the bread and the wine and in the hearts of the communicants making Christ's presence real.

I fear that much of what I have said may have been too intricate and too subtle for many to follow. The best we can do is to come humbly and with faith to the Lord's table ready to receive the blessing he is ready to give. May I however add an appeal to those who have entered into these differing views of the sacrament? Let us be charitable to those who think differently from us and receive them warmly as Christian brothers and sisters. And let the whole Church hold together the ministry of both word and sacrament without the diminution of either. They preserve each other. Without the ministry of the word the presence of God could seem to be brought about by magic. Without the ministry of the sacrament it could seem to be too vague to grasp. And let us pray that by God's 'holy inspiration we may think more things that be good and by his merciful guidance may perform the same through Jesus Christ our Lord'.

21

INCARNATIONAL RELIGION

It was there from the beginning; we have heard it; we have seen it with our own eyes; we looked upon it, and felt it with our own hands; and it is of this we tell.

1 JOHN 1.1 (NEB)

We are now in the middle of November. Those of us who have gardens are busy sweeping up leaves and taking care that our more precious plants are protected against possible frosts. We keep saying to one another, 'It will soon be Christmas', and we begin counting the weeks. Not that we could forget its advent; even our small village has strung up 'fairy lights' across the High Street and the big stores in the towns and cities have started the hectic Christmas sales. So I guess you will half expect me to lament the commercializing of Christmas and how feeble is the general awareness of what it commemorates. I shall refrain from this though I do recall how some years ago I was sitting with my wife at a table in an hotel dining room when some of the guests began to voice their dismay at the pressures Christmas put on people to be ready in time for the great eating and drinking festival. They thought we should all be happier if Christmas were abolished. 'Oh, no', piped up one woman sitting in the corner – I can see her now – 'I think Christmas is *a good idea*!' Apparently she did not connect it with the Christ child. And this took place in Hampstead, not one of the least intellectual parts of London.

1 THE SCOPE OF THE INCARNATION

Now Christmas introduces the subject called the Incarnation. I know it is not a biblical word but what it stands for is deeply biblical, God taking our flesh and living in our world. It was a stupendous event, utterly unique. There has never been anything like it in history though maybe in imagination, and it introduces a principle about life which alters our whole way of thinking about it and our religion too and ways of worship. And it all starts with a baby in a manger at Bethlehem. It all starts with Christmas.

But it doesn't end there. This is the point I am anxious to stress. The whole of Christ's life was the Incarnation, beginning with his conception in Mary's womb; the child in the cradle, yes but also the twelve-year-old boy in the Temple asking questions. This is God in human form. And the virile man recently endowed with the dynamism of God's Spirit striding up and down in the desert agonizing over how he shall employ his powers in the ministry now opening up before him in Galilee. This is God in human form – can you believe it? And that healthy figure pulling a cripple to stand up on his feet. And that commanding preacher able to be heard by five thousand listeners in the open air and hold their attention. And his stinging exposure of religious humbug. And that sagging figure tied to a post, bleeding from the lashes of Roman soldiers because the authorities demanded it. And that slowly dying pain-wracked man on the wooden cross. Yes, and the resurrection on Easter morning and the Ascension. All this from the cradle to the grave, and including both, is the Incarnation. Can you believe it? Can I? This is where we are to look to see God become incarnate, God embodied in a Man, God become a Person (capital 'P'), God made visible.

I hope from this you will catch a glimpse of the size of the subject, its staggering size. One Christmas Day sermon would be wholly inadequate to encompass its scope. Of course there are problems to be faced. You must have sensed them already in what I have been saying. How could Jesus be both God and man? Indeed the very statement blocks off some ears from listening to the Christian Gospel altogether, it begins to sound like nonsense. And if I went into the intricacies of what are called the Christological controversies you would drift off to sleep almost before I started. But there are more than problems here. There are striking insights into the nature of God, mankind and the world in which we live, the sacramental principle, our worship and even our church buildings. Preaching the incarnate Christ is a huge undertaking. I confess I shrink from such a mammoth task but the Church must not shrink from it. There is no lasting Christianity without it.

2 ALERTED TO THE INCARNATE CHRIST

And now I have to say this. Very few people are going to lift their eyes to take note of the incarnate Christ and all that the Incarnation involves as a direct result of what the New Testament tells us about him. Men and women under pressure of either business or pleasure, or both, do not for the most part come to Christian faith in the first place by study of the scriptures, nor by the presentation of doctrines however fundamental. They will only be alerted to take an enquiring interest as a result of contact with individuals or groups of people whose lives have been influenced, shaped or even transformed by responding to the Christian message, a response which is more than intellectual. Then the questions are asked, such as, Why is there a different spirit in this assembly than in a worldly one? Why behind the caring organizations in the community is there most often to be found a Christian foundation group? Why did that man, that woman, go out of their way the other day when I was in desperate need? They were under no obligation whatsoever, and nothing was to be gained by their self-sacrifice. And then this question: What is there about Christ that produces this kind of result and has been producing it for hundreds of years in all manner of places, times and situations? Was Christ simply a man like the rest of us only a great deal better? Who was Jesus? What was he? Why does he still cause people wistfully to wonder in our twentieth-century technological age?

This is the point I am making, the Incarnation calls out for contemporary attention because of what we see around us in our world. It is not an antiquated dogma. It is a living issue. When we observe what Christ has effected, and still effects, we are alerted to ask who he was and is. And no satisfactory answer will be forthcoming unless we take our stand on God incarnate in the Man Jesus, God visible, God as a Person. There is no rest in avoiding this basic truth.

3 A VISIBLE RELIGIOUS FACT

Now a third consideration. The incarnation of Christ makes for an essentially visible religious faith. This is because the incarnate Christ could be heard, seen and touched. Christianity is not simply a spiritual movement, not a thing of the mind only and of a disposition of soul. It organizes among other activities food for famine-stricken peoples, lays water pipes for drought-stricken countries, sends financial relief to disaster areas made so by storm and tempest. Christianity has always been in the forefront of nursing the sick, caring for orphans, yes and for cruelly treated animals, and checking the exploitation of the environment, for it is God's earth. And when people say of certain malpractices that they are 'not Christian' the inference is obvious. Christianity cares. It cares about people's bodies and their physical environment. This is because it is an incarnational religion.

And now its care for the souls of men and women. Here too Christianity is incarnational. It builds churches, indeed the indication that a country is a Christian country is the churches dotted all over it; and they are adorned and may be richly furnished. It would be a poor sort of Christian faith that had not bothered to build a church and was satisfied to have it poorer in appearance than the houses in which the people lived. And the Christian faith supports a live ministry, it presents the Gospel not only in words to be heard but also in sacraments to be seen, chief of which is the Eucharist whose elements are bread and wine able to be seen, tasted and handled. Knock down the churches, strip the churches and you not only show that the faith has died out, you make it die out. To see church spires, to hear church bells, plays a part in ministering the Christian faith, so do choirs, clubs and organizations because – note this – because Christianity is an incarnational religion. Its basis is 'the Word became flesh and dwelt among us'. It ministers the spiritual *through the material*.

Why do we preach the incarnate Christ? Because it is true; God became a visible Person in Christ, this is who he is. People heard him, saw him and touched him, but we also preach him because we cannot have the Christian spirit – and who does not value this? – if we discard the historical events which cover it. There can be no Christianity without Christ, no Christianity without the incarnate Christ, no Christianity without the Spirit mediated by means of the material and physical. And make no mistake, it all begins with Jesus, the historical man, and is only sustained as we keep him in view. And so in our preaching we give time first of all in trying to see him as he was, or as the theologians would put it – first the Jesus of history then the Christ of faith.

22

BODY AND SOUL

If there is a physical body, there is also a spiritual body.

1 CORINTHIANS 15.44 (RSV)

A village usually has a parish church, it is the basis from which the vicar exercises what is technically called his cure of souls delegated to him by the bishop. It also often has a surgery, a modern purpose-built structure where one or two doctors practise, supported by a small staff. Now if you have pains in your stomach, or have a broken leg, you don't see the vicar about the trouble. And if you are worried about a moral tangle in which you have become involved you don't go round to the doctors' surgery. All this sounds so obvious you wonder I bother to mention it. The vicar deals with the soul and the doctor deals with the body. Two parts of us then, the body and the soul. What could be simpler? But is it?

1 EACH PERSON DIVIDED INTO TWO

Nowadays there has come into fairly general use a new word, 'psychosomatic'. This means that no longer is it reckoned that we are all composed of two separate and independent components the physical and the spiritual, the body and the soul, but that every person is a spirit/body complex, a psychosomatic whole being. So the body affects the spirit, and the spirit affects the body. Here is a man who has taken on a new job, the work is demanding and hard and he worries about it, not sleeping at night. He visits his doctor because he has developed digestive trouble. He prescribes pills to take, but the cause of the physical ailment, which is real enough, is not physical but that worry over that new job. Mind affects the body and the body affects the mind. They are connected. They are not separate and independent entities.

Now in the ancient world, the Graeco-Roman world, in which the Christian Gospel was first preached, and where the Church grew up, the prevailing idea was that all human beings were composed of two separate and independent parts, the body and the soul. What was more, the body was perishable but not the soul, the soul was imperishable, it was in fact immortal. So when death overtook the body the soul was set free to dwell in the realm of disembodied spirits. What happened to the body was unimportant for the soul was the superior part of a person, the body the inferior. As a consequence the body could be indulged or abused with impunity, it did not matter, there was no future for it beyond dissolution and decay, for it was merely material, the very antithesis of the spiritual.

To the modern mind this underrating of the physical sounds absurd. We almost worship it. Not only are vast sums of money spent on clothing and cosmetics, almost the whole of life is geared to physical comfort. We expect to eat well and drink well and be entertained well, this is what life is about, and if we discipline ourselves, for example on smoking, it is to enjoy better physical health. All this seems obvious.

But what about the other half of the ancient Graeco-Roman philosophy of life, the half which says that everyone has an immortal soul, utterly distinct from the body, and which survives death, do we jettison this too? Are we bodies and nothing else? Or are we bodies plus minds and so superior to animals? Do we in addition perhaps hang on to the notion that each one of us has an immortal soul, that is, immortal in *its own right*? My guess is that most people today avoid these difficult questions, they sound morbid. Better turn on the television. 'Match of the Day' is more appealing.

2 THE CARE OF THE PHYSICAL

Now I am a Christian preacher and I occupy a Christian pulpit, so I, for one, ought not to dodge the questions, and to be honest, I do not want to dodge them. I conceive it to be my duty to relay as clearly as I can how New Testament Christianity cuts clean across both parts of the Graeco-Roman thought with which it was surrounded. First of all it does not despise the physical body as of little importance able to be indulged and abused with impunity. It is not merely temporary, something inferior with no future, indeed how could Christianity in the light of the Incarnation possibly countenance such a view? God became visible *in a body*. He took a body in which to reveal himself, Christ incarnate; and through a body he died for our sins.

Of course the intellectuals in that old Roman Empire, brought up on Greek philosophy, laughed the whole idea to scorn. How could God, they argued, who is eternal and spiritual be incarnate in that which is temporal and material, namely a human body? The very idea was nonsense. But the fact of Christ, his life, death and resurrection proved to be revolutionary to the thinking of those who faced it; and then our bodies could no longer be counted as mere inferior material fit for exploitation and disposal for Christ had a body. The Christian therefore who believes in the Incarnation, and the Church which is committed to belief in the Incarnation, cannot despise the human body; on the contrary it is bound to care for the physical side of human nature, or to use the old terminology, its ministry is to the body as well as the soul.

Can there be any doubt about this for anyone who takes the life of Jesus, the Incarnate Christ, seriously? How did he fulfil his ministry? In what did his work on earth consist? Was it not in teaching *and healing*? Healing bodies, please note, healing without concern about the cause of the malady whether misfortune, folly or sin. Never for one moment could he be charged with a care only for the souls of men and women and not for their bodies, as if the spiritual only mattered but not the physical. All of which leads us to think that in the Christian reckoning the human body is sacrosanct.

3 A SPIRITUAL BODY

And now my text. No, I haven't forgotten it! The words are to be found in what is called the first letter to the Corinthians in our New Testaments, written to people soaked in that Graeco-Roman culture (about which we have been thinking) but now committed in faith to Christ. They were worried about the fate of their fellow Christians who had died. They said in effect to St Paul through whom they had received the Gospel, 'You talk about the resurrection after death but how are the dead raised up, with what body do they come?' And he did not say, 'Friends, you are mistaken, in the life to come they, we, will not have a body. The body is all over and done with.' No, he said, 'If there is a physical body there is also a spiritual body'. So in the resurrection life we shall not be wraithlike disembodied spirits but spiritual persons with resurrection bodies, bodies which express our individuality as our physical bodies do now; more than that, spiritual bodies related to, but not the same as the bodies we have now for they are physical.

Perhaps this is as far as we can go in our thinking, some would maintain that we have already gone too far. On this, however, I must insist, once we admit the truth of the Incarnation, that is Christ in a human body, having been driven to it by his resurrection, thoughts such as I have raised are bound to follow; and the New Testament bears witness to them, not least in my text, 'If there is a physical body, there is also a spiritual body'. We are body–soul men and women, psychosomatic whole persons, and that we shall ever be, transformed and transfigured on the other side of death.

4 THE INCARNATE CHRIST IS THE KEY

Come back to basics. The key to the life and destiny of us all is Christ, the incarnate Christ, the risen Christ. It is, in the last resort, what we believe about him that determines what we believe about ourselves.

Last November there appeared in our newspapers, as year after year, at Armistice-tide, pictures of war cemeteries in France and Belgium but also in North Africa and Japan. It was impossible not to be impressed by them; first by the veritable sea of headstones marking the graves, a terrible reminder of the awful carnage of two world wars, and then by how beautifully these cemeteries are kept, largely by the War Graves Commission. Nothing is derelict, no grass uncut, no memorial crooked, and here and there a flowering shrub to provide colour. One thing however is strikingly common to all, one simple but stately stone cross lifted up above all the graves in the midst of which it is set. What does it say? It says these men, these women, whose bodies lie here are not lost, there is hope for them all of life on the other side of death, not because they were uncommonly good people, they were not; nor because they had immortal souls anyway, but because of the Christ who was made man, who died and rose again for us all. This is where our hope of life beyond the grave lies, not in ourselves by achievement or by nature but in the Christ whom that white stone cross has been erected to represent.

And so we preach the incarnate Christ crucified and risen. Because he lives we too shall live. Is it any wonder we make much of Easter Day? And here I have to say that for me personally, I see great significance in the empty tomb found by the apostles Peter and John on Easter morning. His body was not there. I do not think it was stolen by thieves or removed by Christ's disciples. It was certainly not left to decompose or to be rubbished; and yet no memorial was erected on this site. The body was cared for and provided for. Is this surprising if, as we believe, God chose a body in which to become incarnate? It would never be left as if of little worth.

At this point I can only say what I believe. I believe Christ's body was transformed in the Resurrection to become a spiritual body for the risen life. And so shall we. 'If there is a physical body [and of course there is] there is also a spiritual body.' So Christ is called 'the first fruits of them that sleep', that is to say he is the first in the general resurrection process, or more accurately perhaps, the leader of it, the *archegos* as the New Testament calls him in the letter to the Hebrews. Can we then repeat the Apostles' Creed with a little more confidence? 'And I look for the resurrection of the dead and the life of the world to come.' And can we hear (when we do) with quickened interest the time honoured words at the administration of the Holy Communion as in the Book of Common Prayer, 'The body of our Lord Jesus Christ which was given for thee, preserve thy body and soul unto eternal life'? Yes, the word 'body' needs interpretation, and mysteries remain. And if we shrink from repeating 'I believe', we might be ready to confess 'We believe'; this is what the Church believes and down the ages has believed, thousands of thousands of believers. Be ready at least then to stand humbly in with them. It is the proper place to stand, it is the safe place, safe for our eternity. I urge you to stand there.

23

THE INCARNATION AND SOCIAL ACTION

He who does what is true comes to the light, that it may be clearly seen that his deeds have been wrought in God.

JOHN 3.21 (RSV)

During the last twenty-five years or so there has been quite an upset in Church circles about the Church and politics. This has come to a head over what is called Liberation theology, particularly in the oppressive social conditions in South America but also causing quite a stir in more than one English parish where the vicar has conceived it to be his duty as a Christian minister to commend specific lines of political action. So the question, Ought the Church to engage in politics?

1 RELIGION AS A PRIVATE SPIRITUAL AFFAIR

Some Christians and some non-Christians have a ready answer, and it is a stout *No*! Religion is a private affair. It is concerned with the relation of the individual soul to God, it is a spiritual matter and has no proper business with social conditions; and if it relaxes this distinctive attitude it will muddy its ministry and grow ineffective.

We need to think carefully about this. First, let it be noted how long and honourable is the separatist approach to religion. Let no one imagine that it has lacked influence or a cutting edge. On the contrary those sects and Christian associations which have been nourished in it have not only displayed remarkable strength but have produced men and women of sterling character. What is more some of them, through individual members, acting responsibly, have exercised valuable influence on government both local and national. Their separatism then does not betoken indifference to community welfare but a conviction that religion is most true to itself when it operates as a private affair. It is this the Church is called to nourish and not to busy itself with social conditions.

Now it is not only some Church people, of whatever denomination that take this view, it represents a general idea in the public. In the General Strike of 1926 Archbishop William Temple led a deputation to the Prime Minister suggesting ways to resolve the dispute on the grounds that it was causing intense suffering to whole communities. The Prime Minister, however, told them bluntly that it was none of their business. 'What would you think?' he snorted, 'if the revision of the Athanasian Creed were entrusted to the Iron and Steel Federation?' The Press at the time took up this rift with some glee leaving the impression that the bishops were a bunch of woolly-headed clerics who would be better employed keeping to their own spiritual concerns.

In the present climate of public opinion there would be supporters in plenty for this view. Contemporary secular thinking – and it colours the prevailing attitude – lays enormous stress on the individual. 'What I do, or don't do, is my afffair, and so long as it does not harm anyone else, is my own business.' Or again, 'Satisfaction in life is to be found in the freedom to do one's own thing'. And yet once again, 'There is no such thing as right or wrong impinging on all, what is wrong for me may be right for you, and vice versa. Everything depends on the individual, his or her temperament, genes, situation or requirement. Who therefore is to say, for example, whether abortion is right or wrong? It concerns the woman's body, it is for her alone to decide.'

When these prevailing ideas are spread to include religion it too has to be regarded as a wholly private and individual affair. If religion helps one but not another, well and good, let them practise it. The situation is no different from one man who finds his satisfaction in golf or one woman whose preference is for bowls. This being the case the Church must not reckon it has any right to concern itself with community affairs. Let it nourish individual piety as much as it wishes appealing to those who 'like that kind of thing'. All of which means it must keep its hands out of politics.

2 INCARNATIONAL RELIGION

And now an opposite point of view, not secular but distinctly religious. It is based on the famous text, 'And the Word became flesh and dwelt among us' (John 1.14). It declares that when God willed to make himself known to us in the utmost clarity possible he came as a Person of flesh and blood. As such, of course, he needed a mother to rear him from childhood, feed him, wash him, and dress him. Till he became an itinerant preacher he had a permanent roof over his head and even thereafter a temporary one. Indifference to these material considerations was impossible. He knew what it was to feel tired, hungry and thirsty. God entered the realm of food, clothes and shelter. He did not leave the revelation of himself to the realm of ideas, philosophies, mysticism or even codes of conduct. His revelation was an embodied one, the spiritual was made known through the material, the invisible through the visible, the abstract through the tangible. This is called incarnational religion and Christianity in practice has to be incarnational because it is rooted and grounded in the incarnate Christ.

So it is that the Christian religion is not content to present it simply as a matter of private piety or a thing of heart and mind, it builds churches of bricks and mortar. It raises spires visible for miles around, it encourages architectural beauty, stained-glass windows and in some places icons. And its worship is not for the most part silent meditation and contemplation but voices lifted up, music, organs, orchestras and movement; and not only that but bread and wine, material substances, in the Holy Communion. The incarnation leads to the sacramental principle. And wherever the Gospel has been preached it has been accompanied by the building of hospitals and schools across the world.

All this means that the Church so long as it is true to the incarnate Christ cannot nourish its religion simply as a private affair of the soul's disposition and relation to God. It has to concern itself also with the environment and the conditions in which we have to live. Marxism to this extent was not wrong when it insisted that the root of evil is not simply in the individual soul but in the circumstances in which the individual is forced to live. The environment counts heavily. Let us not forget that Jesus grew up in a wholesome if humble environment. His was a Jewish way of life and he never forsook it. In it the home was prized to an extent which obtained nowhere else, and the whole structure of life was built on the law and the prophets dedicated to social justice. All this was inherent in the Kingdom of God which he preached. The world is God's world, he is its creator and sustainer, and the servant of God cannot be indifferent to the plight of people denied its benefits. Jesus never was a pauper, and it would not be in his will that any should be.

3 A MIDDLE WAY

What line are we to take then on this vexed question of the Church and politics? There are good men and women representing each of the two views I have outlined. And what am I as a preacher to do? Leave the alternatives and say no more? But this would be weak preaching, weak because it failed to open up what guidance the Scripture may give in the matter, and in particular St John's gospel where the doctrine of the Incarnation has its foundation text, 'And the Word was made flesh'.

Now St John's gospel is nothing if not a spiritual gospel. It opens with a clear statement of God's revelation of himself and of the Word shining as a light in the darkness and enlightening every man that comes into the world. So the gospel tells of the spiritual illumination that can be ours through faith in the incarnate Christ. In and through him we can perceive the truth. According to John 14.6 he said, 'I am the way, and the truth, and the life'. But is this all? It is not. We read in John 3 'he who does the truth comes to the light, that it may be clearly seen that his deeds have been wrought in God'. Note the words '*does* the truth'. So the outcome of the Incarnation of Christ is not only spiritual illumination but practical action. Truth is not only something to be perceived as the Greeks understood it, but something to be done as the Hebrews perceived it to be. All of which is a pointer to what should characterize the Church at all times, not only spiritual culture but practical goodness too. Churches are not to be places isolated from their world and its needs in their concentration on personal piety, they are also to be active in good deeds on behalf of the community, that is welfare. What we have here is not a question of 'Either . . . or' but rather of 'Both . . . and'. This is the interpretation of truth given by St John's gospel and with the whole Old Testament behind it.

But we need to be careful. If the danger of spirituality is separatism and narrowness the danger of engaging in action in the world is worldliness. Jesus warned his disciples that they should be 'in the world' but not 'of the world'. The world is not a neutral area of life. It has its own distinctive spirit which is often inimical to Christ. In it self-interest, self-centredness and greed are rampant. It is a spirit easily caught. The Church can catch it and then it becomes a worldly Church virtually without power.

It is precisely here that the danger for the Church of engaging in politics lies. When it takes up social questions, as on occasions it must, it needs to beware of political methods. It would be wise not to ally itself with any one particular political party. To keep a balance in this is not easy but it is most important if the Church is not to forfeit its distinctive mission. In any case the appropriate action in any social situation that calls for remedies is more complicated than is always realized by the ardent Christian advocates – those clergy whose ministry has of necessity been close to the House of Commons have come to know this.

But can any Church exhibit such a balanced ministry, spiritually alive but not quiescent? Yes, it can, but only if Christ as our light and life is confidently presented; and also as there is a sure grasp of the incarnational basis summed up in the text, 'And the Word was made flesh and dwelt among us'. Then people will see Christianity in action, and faith will be seen both for what it is and what it does. Hear again the words of my text, 'He who does what is true' or as the Greek original has it, 'He who does the truth' – I like the phrase – 'comes to the light, that it may be clearly seen that his deeds have been wrought in God'. Please God, our Church will be one which not only sees the truth and believes, but actually does it.

24

THE INCARNATION AND REVELATION

When in former times God spoke to our forefathers, he spoke in fragmentary and varied fashion through the prophets. But in this final age he has spoken to us in the Son whom he has made heir to the whole universe . . . who is the effulgence of God's splendour and the stamp of God's very being.

HEBREWS 1.1–3 (NEB)

One of the most marked features of the twentieth century is the triumph of science. Most of us experience this for ourselves chiefly in the form of technology and the mulitiplication of gadgets, especially electrical gadgets, not least in the home; and office work has been transformed by computers and word processors. This has gathered momentum in all directions and it is no wonder that the general assumption has come about that science is the final arbiter wherever there is a difference of judgement or opinion. Even products in the shops, if they are to catch on, must be able to advertise that they are made according to a scientific formula. Science sits in the place of supremacy in the world today. Once the formula was 'Rome has spoken the matter is closed', now it is 'science has spoken the matter is closed.'

1 THE RISE OF RATIONALISM

Now I am not so foolish as to 'knock' science. Science is a worthy occupation of man and in the modern world a necessity to be forwarded. Nor do I propose preaching a sermon on 'science versus religion', a wearisome if not pointless battle. I will, however, make three points in passing. Among the professors of science today there are Christian believers, and in general a greater readiness to admit to the mystery of the universe. Science does not know all the answers. Secondly, there is a general awareness that science has not only brought blessings to mankind, it has brought curses, not least in the production of weapons of mass destruction. And thirdly, not even the pure scientist rules his life altogether by science: when he falls in love his choice is not made on any scientific basis whatsoever. Weight and measurement, the chief elements in scientific method, are not the propelling factors why this man is drawn to that woman, and this woman to that man.

No, science is not the undisputed monarch, nevertheless rationalism, which is akin to it, is the dominant mood of the present day. Reason is paramount. Not that this is altogether new. The eighteenth century was the Age of Reason in Europe, especially in what is called the Enlightenment in Germany; and it affected the Christian religion chiefly through Protestantism. Until that time what we knew about God was reckoned to come by means of revelation, that is by the disclosure of God himself, not by human reason. Gradually however some truths were thought to derive from revelation and some from reason, especially reason about the natural world. Then little by little reason took over more and more with nothing that could not be substantiated by it being acceptable to the educated man. This represents the rationalistic mood of today, and even where it does not abolish religion altogether it reshapes it. So where does this leave us with regard to revelation? Can we accept the idea of a revealed religion any more, and if so how? This is my subject.

2 REVEALED RELIGION

Now the Bible is downright on this subject. Not surprisingly therefore it comes under attack in the modern world declaring as it does that God reveals himself through speech and action. Over and over again the phrase occurs, 'And God said', and again and again he is described as acting for his people notably in bringing up the Hebrews from their slavery in Egypt and also sending them into exile in Babylon. So we read in the Bible of the word of God and of the mighty acts of God. We read too of the agents through which he accomplished his purposes, prophets like Isaiah and kings like David. So the Bible introduces a revealed religion, a religion originating from God not man. Its knowledge of God is not the reward of human discovery nor is the religion derived from it of total human construction. To put it crudely, biblical religion descends from above, it does not rise up from below. The one represents revelation, the other reason.

The New Testament accepts the Old Testament presentation and builds on it. Listen to the text from Hebrews 1.1–3, 'When in former times God spoke to our forefathers, he spoke in fragmentary and varied fashion through the prophets. But in this final age he has spoken to us in the Son . . . who is the effulgence of God's splendour and the stamp of God's very being.' God then is revealed *supremely* in Christ. He is revealed in the incarnate Christ. He is revealed in the Man Jesus in what he was seen to be, to say and to do. This means that the supreme revelation of God is in a Person, not a religious system, nor a moral code, nor a set of doctrines but a Person; and because this is the supreme revelation all revelation must be tested by it.

But are we prepared to accept the supremacy of Christ? This is the question. The supremacy of Christ is not an assessment to be proved by a process of reason, in the last resort it is a judgement of faith. Reason, therefore, however highly it may rate Jesus stops short of the confession that he is God incarnate. And so the concept of revelation falls to the ground. In this matter therefore everything turns on the interpretation we give to the life and ministry of Jesus. The Christian Church has traditionally seen it in the light of his resurrection and so counted that life and ministry as the revelation of God, supreme because incarnate, and has noted at various places in it disclosure points of revelation in the way the Gospel writers have related it, notably the Baptism and Transfiguration. This dimension can however be rationalized, some would claim, explained away. Then we are left with a Jesus noble indeed, for he even accepted death rather than sacrifice his principles, but not God incarnate. What is more the 'happy ending' of the resurrection distorts the story of Jesus because life as we know it does not have happy endings, they are not the lot of goodness in this world as we know it.

The trouble with the rationalistic approach to the Bible countering as it does the basic idea of revelation is that it removes the *religious* value of the Bible for us. What we struggling men and women need, and why we turn to religion at all, is a power beyond us to guide, succour and indeed save us. Otherwise why bother with it more than with other stories of human endeavour? However highly, therefore, we may value the Bible for the ancient history it provides and for the excellence of its literature, at the end of the day its character as revelation is what places it in a class by itself.

Now none of this means that reason is to be curtailed in our handling of the Bible and in our approach to religion. The very fact that the supreme revelation of God is in a Person, the incarnate Christ, requires that reason be critically though reverently applied to the Bible and the doctrines based on it. The Bible as a book is not the revelation of God, it is the human record of that revelation the ultimate of which is the incarnate Christ. As the writer of the Espistle to the Hebrews puts it (1.3) 'He is the effulgence of God's splendour and the stamp of God's very being'. And as St Paul expressed it in his letter to the Colossians (2.9): 'For it is in Christ that the complete being of the Godhead dwells embodied'. These are not confessions arrived at without the experience of reason but they are not the product of pure reason, their basis is revelation, the revelation in the incarnate Christ, in the light of which all that is presented as revelation is to be measured. And if this applies to the Bible it applies also to the doctrines proclaimed by the Church. It is not doctrines that have been revealed by God and which shape our religion but the Person of God incarnate, the Lord Jesus Christ.

3 THE DOCTRINE OF THE TRINITY

Let no one suppose, however, that doctrines are irrelevant or unimportant. The doctrine of the Trinity is very much a case in point. It can be deduced from passages of Scripture. For example when Jesus is reported (John 14.15) as saying, 'I will ask the Father, and he will give you another to be your Advocate, who will be with you for ever – the Spirit of truth', so then Father, Son and Holy Spirit. Similarly the benediction at the close of St Paul's second letter to the Corinthians (13.14), 'The grace of the Lord Jesus Christ, and the love of God, and fellowship in the Holy Spirit, be with you all'. The doctrine is, however, nowhere set down in *formal* terms in the New Testament. What we must appreciate is that this doctrine originated because of the Incarnation and without it no one would have proceeded beyond 'I believe in one God, the Father Almighty, Maker of heaven and earth'. Faith in the incarnate Son of God eventually leads to a Trinitarian faith, God the Father, God the Son, God the Holy Spirit.

Unless you happen to be a trained theologian I do not recommend you to attempt to puzzle out how this triune Godhead is to be explained and even if you are, remember that the Godhead is the ultimate mystery. Rather than worry over how the three Persons can possibly be understood as we understand persons or whether they are three modes of existence, it is better for most of us to be content with a trinity of *our experience* of God leaving aside what God is in himself – God the creator, God the Saviour, God the

Holy Spirit, the means of our fellowship with God and with one another.

Finally, forgive me, if this sermon ending this series has been hard to follow and devoid of illustrations, almost like a house destitute of windows, but the subject handled is a profound one and I have been afraid of making it trite. We began by giving our attention to science. In our knowledge of God science cannot carry us very far, and rationalism can remove God altogether from serious regard. In our knowledge of God faith is indispensable, faith evoked by the incarnate Christ. And I would have you notice that the Church's Creeds do not begin with 'I believe *that*' but 'I believe *in*', signifying trust not assent to propositions. 'I believe in God the Father . . . I believe in Jesus Christ . . . I believe in the Holy Spirit.' In the last resort when we have done all our thinking, all our reasoning, all our discussing we can but trust in the God revealed in the incarnate Christ. Our safety lies there. And so we proclaim him. We preach the incarnate Christ.